Photography by Issy Croker

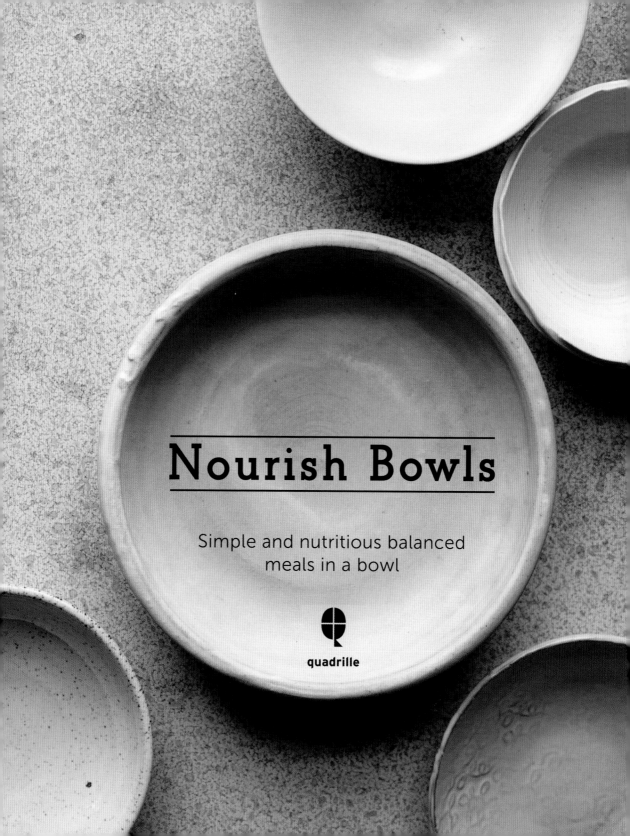

Nourish Bowls

Simple and nutritious balanced
meals in a bowl

quadrille

CONTENTS

INTRODUCTION

NOURISH BOWLS are made from the heart, comforting, fulfilling, health-giving, and delicious. They are everything you need in a bowl to nourish your body and mind, whether you have just a few minutes to pull together a meal, want to try out new ingredients and flavours, or help your body recover optimally after a workout.

From rice and noodle bowls in Japan, to the Korean bibimbap and the Swedish hygge, or 'hug in a bowl', cultures all over the world have traditional bowl-based recipes. And now it has become a simple way to bring together a nourishing meal, including all the key nutritional elements, to hold in our hands, however hectic our lives. Putting together the bowl feels like an act of mindfulness in itself, combining natural, flavourful ingredients, textures and colours, vibrancy, and vitality.

A nourish bowl can be quick and simple to prepare, with many of the elements being included raw. There is so much variety possible, with countless wholesome combinations of vegetables, greens, grains, plant-based proteins, meat, or fish. From breakfast bowls that combine pear with kale in a smoothie served with cinnamon granola, or miso oats with spinach and a poached egg, to a citrus and fennel salad bowl with goat cheese and toasted quinoa, a brown rice Buddha bowl, and hearty bowls like mushroom rye risotto with baby chard and wet walnuts, or chilli chicken with corn and avocado salsa, black quinoa, and zesty sour cream, we hope to give you plenty of inspiration for creating your own health-giving and delicious nourish bowls.

Go bold with your flavours and combinations, layer up your grains, protein, and leafy greens, then scatter over a few toasted seeds, roasted sweet potato crisps, or a little turmeric dressing. Whether you keep it simple with some roasted veggies, homemade hummus, salad leaves, and a few alfalfa sprouts or fancy some smoked fish with lentils and a big bunch of greens, thinking about the simple elements of the nourish bowl will deliver a nutrient-packed meal every time.

Over the seasons, you can adapt your nourish bowls to the ingredients nature provides. During the summer, add more raw vegetables and leaves, while in the colder months roasted root vegetables are the perfect addition with a red lentil hummus or smashed avocado with lime. There is an amazing variety of grains now available to suit any nourish bowl, especially in your local health food store, including different coloured quinoa, buckwheat, freekeh, millet, and various 'groats', which are the whole grains of foods we might be more used to seeing as flour or flakes, such as oat and rye groats. These add so much variety of taste and texture. There are also lots of seeds in all different sizes, from the tiny chia to flax, sesame, hemp, and pumpkin. As seeds they are literally packed with nutrients.

You might find some of the recipes are a little more creative than others, for when you want to try something new and adventurous. There are lots of ideas for elements that you can make ahead and keep handy in the refrigerator, such as dressings, pickles, and pastes. Don't feel you have to bake your own soda bread or make your own ricotta, we have simply included as many recipes as possible for when you might fancy giving these things a try. In most instances, the recipes make enough for one serving. If you want to share a nourish bowl with friends, then multiply the quantites by the number of servings required.

MAKING YOUR NOURISH BOWL

The basic concept of the nourish bowl is to include all the nutritional elements you ideally need in one meal: protein (whether it be plant-based, dairy, fish or meat), seasonal fruits or vegetables, leafy greens, complex carbohydrates, healthy fats, and any optional extras you fancy like a dressing, a few nuts, or seeds. Let your imagination go.

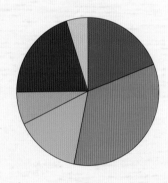

● PROTEIN
aim for 25 per cent of your bowl to be made up by protein

● VEGETABLES & FRUIT
vegetables, fruits, or a combination of the two should form the largest proportion of your bowl

● LEAFY GREENS
include a large handful of leafy green in every bowl

● COMPLEX CARBOHYDRATES
ensure that healthy carbs occupy 25 per cent of your bowl

● HEALTHY FATS
if possible make about 10 per cent of your bowl include a healthy fat

● TOPPINGS & DRESSINGS
add any optional extras to add extra bite or flavour

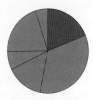

● PROTEINS

Protein is a key building block for our muscles, bones, cartilage, skin, and blood. It helps our body carry out all the day-to-day general repair work, especially when we have an active lifestyle. Protein also keeps us fuller for longer as it takes the body more time and effort to break down its nutrients. There are plenty of plant-based proteins to choose from, as well as dairy, eggs, meat, and fish.

PLANT-BASED
- Tofu
- Beans (including aduki, borlotti, broad or fava, edamame, mung, and soybeans)
- lentils and pulses (including beluga lentils, split peas, green or Puy lentils, and chickpeas or garbanzo beans)
- Quinoa
- Nuts
- Seeds (including hemp seeds)

DAIRY
- Cheese (including goat and sheep cheese)
- Yogurt
- Labneh
- Kefir

FISH & SHELLFISH
- Cod (use sustainable whenever possible)
- Crab
- Crayfish
- Haddock
- Sea bass
- Mackerel
- Mussels
- Salmon
- Shrimps
- Squid
- Trout

ANIMAL SOURCES
- Eggs
- Meat (including chicken, turkey duck, lamb, pork, beef – use organic whenever possible)
- Game birds (including quail and pheasant)

● VEGETABLES & FRUITS

Add extra colour and therefore nutrients to your bowl with whatever veggies or fruits you fancy. You might want to add slices of citrus fruit to your salad bowl, or some grated raw carrot, cucumber ribbons, shredded or fermented cabbage.

VEGETABLES
- Asparagus
- Aubergine (egg plant)
- Beetroot (beet)
- Brassicas (including broccoli, sprouts, cauliflower, & kohlrabi)
- Capsicum (including bell pepper and chili pepper)
- Carrot
- Celeriac (celery root)
- Courgette (zucchini)
- Cucumber
- Jerusalem artichoke
- Legumes (including peas and mange tout)
- Onion
- Radish
- Samphire
- Sea vegetables (including sea spaghetti, nori flakes, sea salad)
- Spring onion (scallion)
- Squash (including butternut and pumpkin)
- Tomato

FRUIT
- Apple
- Banana
- Berries (including acai, blackberries, blueberries, loganberries, raspberries, and strawberries)
- Citrus (including clementine, grapefruit, and orange)
- Grapes
- Melon
- Pear
- Watermelon

MUSHROOMS
In a food group of their own, mushrooms are thought to be particularly beneficial to health.
- Enoki
- Girolle
- Oyster
- Porcini
- Shiitake

● LEAFY GREENS

Your leafy greens of choice form the base of the nourish bowl, packed with anti-ageing, energy-fuelling antioxidants, vitamins, and minerals.

- Asian greens (including bok choy or pak choi, tatsoi)
- Cavolo nero
- Collard greens
- Dandelion leaves
- Kale
- Lambs lettuce
- Micro greens
- Mustard greens
- Pea shoots
- Purple sprouting broccoli
- Rainbow chard
- Rocket
- Romaine
- Savoy cabbage
- Spinach
- Spring greens
- Swiss chard
- Turnip tops
- Watercress
- Wild garlic leaves

● COMPLEX CARBOHYDRATES

Complex carbohydrates provide the bulk of the energy we need. Being 'complex' means that the carbohydrates release their energy gradually, unlike sugars that cause a sudden spike, quickly followed by a low—the 'afternoon slump' most of us have experienced at one time or another.

   These starchy carbohydrates often contain plenty of fibre, essential for our all-important gut health. They also tend to be less energy dense than other foods, such as fats, in that they contain less calories for the volume of food, so they are perfect for adding to any nourish bowl.

- Barley
- Beans (contains both protein and carbohydrate)
- Brown rice
- Buckwheat
- Bulgur
- Corn
- Couscous
- Farro
- Fermented rice
- Freekeh
- Fregola
- Jasmine rice
- Millet
- Noodles (choose either buckwheat or rice noodles)
- Oats
- Peas
- Polenta (cornmeal)
- Quinoa (contains both protein and carbohydrate)
- Red rice
- Rye
- Spelt (pearled)
- Sticky rice
- Sweet potato
- Wheatberries

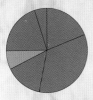

● HEALTHY FATS

Healthy fats come in the form of MUFAs, PUFAs, and Omegas. We now know that far from making us fat, these healthy fats actually reduce harmful cholesterol in the body, are anti-inflammatory, and boost our brainpower. There are lots of natural ingredients that contain healthy fats, especially avocado, nuts and seeds, olive oil, and coconut oil.

• Avocado
• Coconut oil
• Extra virgin olive oil
• Oily fish (including salmon, mackerel, and tuna)
• Olives
• Nuts (including almonds, hazelnuts, and pecans)
• Nut and seed oils
• Seeds (including flax, hemp, pumpkin, and sesame)

● TOPPINGS & DRESSINGS

You might want to scatter over some seeds for a little extra nourishment and crunch, or add turmeric, lemon, or apple cider vinegar to a dressing to add bonus benefits.

TOPPINGS
- Fresh herbs
- Furikake (a Japanese seasoning of black and white sesame seeds and nori flakes)
- Kimchi (see page 155)
- Miso
- Mustard
- Nutritional yeast
- Pickles (see page 155)
- Sauerkraut
- Toasted seeds
- Tamari

DRESSINGS
- Apple cider vinegar
- Buttermilk dressing (see page 155)
- Preserved lemon dressing (see page 155)
- Tahini dressing (page 155)
- Turmeric dressing (page 155)

POWDERS
There are a number of concentrated natural food powders now available that you might experiment with adding to your nourish bowls. They tend to be extremely nutrient-dense.
- Beetroot (beet)
- Cacao
- Lucuma
- Matcha
- Spirulina
- Wheatgrass

BREAKFAST BOWLS

We've included plenty of breakfast bowl ideas to fire up your metabolism in the morning. Give yourself the best start to the day with a power smoothie, savoury porridge, or the classic combination of eggs, avocado, and kale.

●●● CINNAMON GRANOLA
●●● PEAR & KALE SMOOTHIE
● COCONUT YOGURT
● MIXED SEEDS & DRIED BERRIES

FOR THE CINNAMON GRANOLA Preheat the oven to 140°C/275°F/ gas mark 1. Line a baking tray with baking parchment. Melt 85g (3 oz./ 8 tbsp) coconut oil and 2 tbsp honey over a low heat. Place 100g (3½ oz./1 cup) uncooked jumbo rolled oats, 20g (¾ oz./2 tbsp) quinoa, 20g (¾ oz./3 tbsp) pumpkin seeds, 20g (¾ oz./2 tbsp) flaxseeds, 40g (1½ oz./¼ cup) roughly chopped almonds, 20g (¾ oz./¼ cup) dried cranberries and 1 tsp ground cinnamon (or more to taste) in a mixing bowl. Add the melted coconut oil and honey and stir well, until coated in the oil. Tip onto the prepared tray and spread the mixture out evenly. Bake in the oven for 50 minutes, stirring a couple of times to make sure it doesn't stick and burn. Remove from the oven and leave to cool for 10 minutes. If you want extra-crunchy granola, turn the oven off and leave the door open, with the granola still inside.

FOR THE PEAR & KALE SMOOTHIE Blend together 1 pear, quartered and cored, a large handful of kale, tough stalks removed and leaves shredded, some coconut water and, if you need a little more sweetness, 1 tsp runny honey. (If your blender isn't powerful enough for raw kale, steam for a few minutes first.)

TO ASSEMBLE YOUR BOWL Add the pear and kale smoothie to the bowl, then add 3 heaped tablespoonfuls of granola. Top with a spoonful of dairy-free coconut yogurt or natural (plain) yogurt, pumpkin seeds, shelled hemp seeds, and dried cranberries.

- POACHED EGG
- MISO ONION OAT GROATS
- SPINACH
- SESAME SEEDS
- MIXED CRESS LEAVES

FOR THE MISO OAT GROATS AND SPINACH Soak 55g (2 oz./⅓ cup) oat groats in cold water overnight, then rinse and drain thoroughly. Heat 1 tsp olive oil in a saucepan and gently fry 1 chopped small onion or shallot for a few minutes, before stirring through the drained oat groats. Mix 1 tsp white or brown miso paste with a little just-boiled water to loosen, before adding about 300ml (10 fl oz./1¼ cups) just-boiled water. Stir and then add to the oats. Bring to the boil, lower the heat and simmer gently until the oats are cooked (oat groats keep a bite to them), about 15 minutes. Stir through 2 large handfuls of spinach.

FOR THE POACHED EGG Bring a saucepan of water to a bare simmer, crack an egg into a cup then slide it into the water. Poach for 3–4 minutes, depending on how soft you like your egg, then remove with a slotted spoon.

TO ASSEMBLE YOUR BOWL Spoon the miso onion oat groats into the bowl and top with the poached egg. Scatter over some black or white sesame seeds and a small handful of mixed cress leaves.

●●● BERRY & SPINACH SMOOTHIE

● SEASONAL FRUITS

● SPINACH

●● PECAN GRANOLA

● MIXED SEEDS

● BEE POLLEN

FOR THE PECAN GRANOLA Preheat the oven to 140°C/275°F/gas mark 1. Line a baking tray with baking parchment. Mix 1 tsp vanilla extract with 85g (3 oz./8 tbsp) melted coconut oil. Place 100g (3½ oz./1 cup) uncooked jumbo rolled oats, 1 tsp ground ginger, 55g (2 oz./½ cup) pecan halves, 55g (2 oz./⅓ cup) dried cranberries, 40g (1½ oz./⅓ cup) roughly chopped hazelnuts and 30g (1 oz./¼ cup) pumpkin seeds in a mixing bowl. Add the melted coconut oil and stir well, until coated in the oil. Tip onto the prepared tray and spread the mixture out evenly. Bake in the oven for 50 minutes, stirring a couple of times to make sure it doesn't stick and burn. Remove from the oven and leave to cool for 10 minutes. If you want extra-crunchy granola, turn the oven off and leave the door open, with the granola still inside.

FOR THE BERRY & SPINACH SMOOTHIE Blend together 1 tbsp acai berry powder, 1 tsp lucuma powder, ½ frozen sliced banana, a handful of blueberries, 1 tbsp almond butter, a large handful of spinach and some almond milk.

TO ASSEMBLE YOUR BOWL Add the berry & spinach smoothie to the bowl, then top with 3 heaped spoonfuls of granola. Top with fresh seasonal fruit, such as sliced figs, strawberries, redcurrants, raspberries, and blueberries, then sprinkle over a mix of flax, sesame, chia, and hemp seeds, with some bee pollen.

- SCRAMBLED EGGS
- RADICCHIO
- COCONUT KALE
- SODA BREAD
- AVOCADO
- SESAME SEEDS

FOR THE SODA BREAD (If baking your own) Preheat the oven to 200°C/400°F/gas mark 6. Sift 255g (9 oz./1¾ cups) spelt or kamut flour, 1 tsp bicarbonate of soda and ½ tsp sea salt into a large bowl, and mix. Form a well in the middle and gradually pour in 300ml (10½ fl. oz/1⅓ cups) natural (plain) yogurt while stirring. You are looking for a soft dough, just beyond sticky. On a lightly floured surface, knead the dough lightly for just a minute to make a loose ball. (It won't feel springy because there is no yeast.) Be quick so that the bicarbonate of soda is working as you put the bread in the oven, and don't worry about any cracks, as they will make the bread lovely and crusty. Place the dough on a floured baking tray and dust generously with flour. Cut a deep cross in the top then bake for about 30 minutes. Check the loaf sounds hollow when tapped on the base, and if it doesn't, continue to bake and check again. Remove from the oven when ready and allow to cool.

FOR THE COCONUT KALE Remove the woody stalks from a large handful of kale, then roughly chop the leaves and rinse well. Heat a little coconut oil in a wok or sauté pan and add the kale; the residual water will help to soften the kale as it cooks, which should take about 5 minutes, stirring occasionally.

FOR THE SCRAMBLED EGGS Whisk 2 eggs in a small bowl, then heat a non-stick pan, melt a little butter in the pan and add the eggs. Keep stirring over a low heat until you have soft scrambled eggs. Season to taste.

TO ASSEMBLE YOUR BOWL Add the kale and scrambled eggs to the bowl, with 1 sliced avocado alongside. Sprinkle with sesame or hemp seeds, add a large handful of raddichio leaves, then serve with a slice of toasted soda bread.

●●●●● BANANA, CUCUMBER, AVOCADO, & MINT SMOOTHIE
● QUINOA FLAKES
● BLACK GRAPES

FOR THE BANANA,CUCUMBER, AVOCADO & MINT SMOOTHIE Place 2 tbsp quinoa flakes in a bowl with enough water to cover, and leave to soak for 30 minutes. Blend together ½ frozen sliced banana, ¼ cucumber, chopped, 1 small peeled, de-stoned avocado, a small handful of mint leaves, roughly chopped, the soaked quinoa flakes, and 150ml (5 fl. oz./²/₃ cup) coconut water.

TO ASSEMBLE YOUR BOWL Add the smoothie to the bowl and top with a small handful of halved black grapes (or blueberries) and sprinkle over a few extra quinoa flakes.

- CODDLED EGG
- BABY CAULIFLOWER
- BABY KALE
- FREGOLA SHAKSHUKA

FOR THE CAULIFLOWER Preheat the oven to 230°C/450°F/gas mark 8. Toss 2 baby cauliflowers in a little olive oil and salt, add to a roasting tin or dish and roast in the oven for 20–25 minutes, until golden brown.

FOR THE SHAKSHUKA Heat 2 tbsp olive oil in a heavy-based shallow pan. Add ½ chopped red onion and sauté for about 8 minutes before creating a space in the pan and adding ¼ tsp ground cumin, ¼ tsp ground coriander, ¼ tsp ground turmeric, ½ tsp paprika, ½ tsp fennel seeds and a pinch of chilli flakes. After 30 seconds or so, stir the spices through the onion and add 1 sliced red bell pepper, 100g (3½ oz./about 8–9) vine cherry tomatoes, ½ tbsp tomato paste, and ½ tsp coconut sugar. Stir, bring to a simmer, and cook for about 30 minutes.

FOR THE FREGOLA Cook 50g (2 oz./¼ cup) fregola according to the instructions on the packet, drain, and add to the shakshuka.

FOR THE EGG Make a hollow in the shakshuka and fregola mixture and crack an egg into it. Return to a simmer and cover with a lid for about 5 minutes, until the egg is cooked with the yolk still runny.

TO ASSEMBLE YOUR BOWL Add the roast cauliflower to the pan and scatter over a generous handful of baby kale leaves.

KEFIR, BANANA, & CACAO SMOOTHIE
ALMOND GRANOLA
POMEGRANATE SEEDS
BEETROOT CRISPS

FOR THE ALMOND GRANOLA Preheat the oven to 140°C/275°F/gas mark 1. Line a baking tray with baking parchment. Melt 85g (3 oz./8 tbsp) coconut oil in a pan. Place 100g (3½ oz./1 cup) uncooked jumbo rolled oats, 1 tsp ground ginger, 1 tbsp beetroot (beet) powder, 55g (2 oz./½ cup) dried blueberries and 55g (2 oz./⅓ cup) roughly chopped almonds in a mixing bowl. Add the melted coconut oil and stir well, until coated in the oil. Tip onto the prepared tray and spread the mixture out evenly. Bake in the oven for 50 minutes, stirring a couple of times to make sure it doesn't stick and burn. Remove from the oven and leave to cool for 10 minutes. If you want extra-crunchy granola, turn the oven off and leave the door open, with the granola still inside.

FOR THE BEETROOT CRISPS Scrub and thinly slice raw beetroot (beet), ideally with a mandolin, spread the slices out in a single layer on an oven tray, and bake in the oven at 180°C/350°F/gas mark 4 for 10–15 minutes, until crisp. Stored in an airtight container, the beetroot crisps will last 2–3 days.

FOR THE KEFIR, BANANA & CACAO SMOOTHIE Blend ½ frozen sliced banana, 1 tbsp cacao powder, ½ tsp matcha powder (optional), a handful of spinach, ½ peeled and roughly chopped avocado and 100ml (3½ fl. oz./⅓ cup) kefir, adding a little water or coconut water if needed to obtain the right consistency.

TO ASSEMBLE YOUR BOWL Add the smoothie to the base of the bowl. Top with a few heaped spoonfuls of granola, some beetroot crisps, and a spoonful of pomegranate seeds.

SMOKED HADDOCK OMELETTE
SPINACH, HERBS, & CRESS
FARRO
YUZU HOLLANDAISE

FOR THE FARRO Cook 30g (1 oz./¼ cup) farro (wheat berries) according to the packet instructions and drain.

FOR THE MIXED HERBS & SPINACH Chop a handful of spinach with some mixed herbs and cress.

FOR THE YUZU HOLLANDAISE Melt 100g (3½ oz./7 tbsp) unsalted butter and skim off any white solids. Keep the butter warm while you bring a pan of water to a simmer. Place a heatproof bowl over the simmering water pan, and in the bowl whisk together 2 egg yolks and 1 tsp white wine vinegar until you have any airy foam (sabayon). Remove the bowl from the pan and whisk in a little of the melted butter, then replace the bowl over the pan and whisk constantly. Repeat until all the butter has been whisked in and the texture is similar to mayonnaise. Add a little yuzu (or lemon juice), salt and freshly ground black pepper to taste.

FOR THE SMOKED HADDOCK Bring a small pan of milk seasoned with a little sea salt to a simmer, add 140g (5 oz.) un-dyed smoked haddock fillet and poach for 6–8 minutes until soft and flaking. Remove from the heat.

FOR THE OMELETTE Gently beat 2 large eggs using a fork. Heat a medium frying pan until really hot, adding 1 tsp olive oil. Add the beaten eggs and leave for about 5 seconds so that the mixture begins to bubble up, then start to pull the cooked edges into the centre and tip the runny middle to the edges. When the surface is still a little runny, fold over the omelette and remove from the heat.

TO ASSEMBLE YOUR BOWL Serve the omelette topped with the drained poached haddock, flaked into pieces, the farro, herbs, and spinach, and a spoonful of yuzu hollandaise.

●●●● GREEN PROTEIN SMOOTHIE
●●● PUMPKIN SPICED OATS
● MIXED SEEDS
● DRIED BERRIES

FOR THE PUMPKIN SPICED OATS Put 55g (2 oz./½ cup) rolled oats, 100ml (3½ fl. oz./⅓ cup) almond milk, and 100ml (3½ fl. oz./⅓ cup) water in a pan and bring to the boil. Reduce to a simmer and stir in 1 tbsp pumpkin purée, 1 tbsp maple syrup or runny honey, ¼ tsp ground cinnamon, and a generous pinch of ground cloves. Simmer gently for about 10 minutes, stirring every now and then. Let stand for a couple for minutes with the lid on.

FOR THE GREEN PROTEIN SMOOTHIE Blend ½ peeled and roughly chopped avocado, a handful of kale, tough stalks removed and leaves shredded (or use spinach), ⅓ cucumber, roughly chopped, 2 tbsp shelled hemp seeds and as much apple juice as you need to achieve the right consistency.

TO ASSEMBLE YOUR BOWL Spoon the spiced oats into the bowl and add a sprinkling of mixed seeds, dried cranberries, and goji berries. Serve the green protein smoothie on the side for the ultimate power breakfast.

- SPICED FRUIT & FETA SALAD
- WATERMELON GAZPACHO
- BABY CHARD LEAVES
- QUINOA FLAKES
- EXTRA VIRGIN OLIVE OIL
- TOASTED QUINOA FLAKES

FOR THE SPICED FRUIT & FETA SALAD Preheat the oven to 200°C/400°F /gas mark 6. Chop ¼ papaya and ¼ small watermelon into cubes. Mix in a bowl with 1 tsp Chinese five-spice and ½ tsp nigella seeds, then spread out on a non-stick baking tray and roast for 10 minutes. Set aside to cool to room temperature, then mix with a handful of fresh blueberries and 30g (1 oz./¼ cup) feta, cut into small cubes.

FOR THE WATERMELON GAZPACHO Place 2 tbsp quinoa flakes in a bowl with enough water to cover, and leave to soak for 30 minutes. Blend together 200g (7 oz./1 cup) chopped watermelon flesh, 90ml (3 fl. oz. /6 tbsp) passata (strained tomatoes), the soaked quinoa flakes, a dash each of Tabasco and Worcestershire sauce, and a little extra virgin olive oil. Season to taste with sea salt and freshly ground black pepper.

TO ASSEMBLE YOUR BOWL Cover the base of the bowl with toasted quinoa flakes and a good handful of baby chard leaves or amaranth. Add the gazpacho and top with the roasted fruit and feta salad. Drizzle over some extra virgin olive oil.

LIGHT BOWLS

These are everyday bowls that you can mix and match, tweaking the ingredients according to what is in season. Never be bored by salads again and discover some new flavours to try out. Lots of these ideas work in a lunchbox so you can enjoy them either at work or out and about.

QUINOA-DUSTED POLENTA
CORNO PEPPER
PICKLED GREENS
SHEEP CHEESE

FOR THE PICKLED GREENS Roughly chop a bunch of spring greens and place in a heatproof bowl. Bring 200ml (6¾ fl. oz./¾ cup + 1 tbsp) water to the boil, leave for a few minutes, and then add 100ml (3½ fl. oz./⅓ cup) apple cider vinegar. Pour the vinegar mixture over the greens. Leave to marinate overnight.

FOR THE QUINOA-DUSTED POLENTA Pour 100ml (3½ fl. oz./⅓ cup) milk into a small pan, add a large rosemary sprig and 1 peeled garlic clove and gently bring to just below simmering point. Remove from the heat and set aside to infuse for several hours, or overnight. Strain the infused milk into a medium pan and add 100ml (3½ fl. oz./⅓ cup) water. Place over a high heat and pour in 55g (2 oz./⅓ cups) quick-cook polenta (cornmeal), whisking as you do so to separate the grains. Bring to the boil then reduce to a simmer, stirring until it reaches a creamy consistency. Line a rectangular or square plastic container with baking parchment rubbed with oil. Pour in the polenta, cover the surface of the polenta tightly with plastic wrap, prick with the tip of a sharp knife, and leave to set overnight. Tip out the set polenta and cut into cubes. Mix together some dry polenta and black quinoa, then roll the cubes in the mixture to coat on all sides. Heat some coconut oil in a frying pan and fry the polenta cubes until golden on all sides.

FOR THE CORNO PEPPER To make your own (or you can buy them in jars) cook a Romano pepper directly over the gas flame or under a hot grill, until blackened on all sides. Place in a bowl and cover until cool, when you can easily peel off the charred skin. Cut the flesh into strips.

TO ASSEMBLE YOUR BOWL Add some pickled greens, polenta cubes and the strips of pepper to the bowl, then top with shavings of hard sheep cheese, or Parmesan.

- CHICKPEAS
- CUCUMBER & APPLE
- MIXED SALAD LEAVES
- FREGOLA
- HONEY MUSTARD DRESSING

FOR THE MIXED SALAD LEAVES & CHICKPEAS Chop ½ cucumber into batons, put into a large mixing bowl with 2 large handfuls of mixed salad leaves, and 100g (3½ oz./¾ cup) cooked chickpeas (garbanzo beans).

FOR THE FREGOLA (Or use buckwheat for a gluten-free alternative.) Cook 40g (1½ oz./scant ½ cup) fregola according to the instructions on the packet. Drain, leave to cool, then add to the mixing bowl.

FOR THE HONEY MUSTARD DRESSING Mix together ½ tsp freshly grated or ground turmeric, 2 tsp pickled mustard seeds, and pickling liquid (see page 155), 1 tsp runny honey, and 3 tbsp extra virgin olive oil. Pour a little of the dressing over the salad and mix everything gently together.

TO ASSEMBLE YOUR BOWL Spoon the dressed salad into the bowl and top with 1 finely sliced apple. Serve the remaining dressing alongside, adding extra to taste.

BROAD BEAN BIGILLA
BABY VEGETABLES
BEETROOT LEAVES
MIXED QUINOA
CITRUS-INFUSED OLIVE OIL
RYE CRACKERS

FOR THE BROAD BEAN BIGILLA Blanch 85g (3 oz./¾ cups) shelled and peeled fresh broad (fava) beans in boiling water for 1 minute, then process them with ½ garlic clove, a good pinch of sea salt, a generous splash of extra virgin olive oil, ½ deseeded and finely chopped green chili pepper, and plenty of lemon juice. Mix in 1 heaped tbsp Greek yogurt.

FOR THE MIXED QUINOA Cook 55g (2 oz./⅓ cup) mixed quinoa according to the instructions on the packet. Put into a small side bowl.

FOR THE BABY VEGETABLES & BEETROOT LEAVES Choose a mixture of baby vegetables, including carrots, radishes, and beetroot (beets), clean well and chop, vertically where appropriate, into bite-sized pieces. Reserve the beetroot leaves (beet greens) to add to your bowl. Season.

TO ASSEMBLE YOUR BOWL Spoon the bigilla into the bowl and add the beetroot leaves and baby vegetables. Drizzle with some citrus-infused oil (see page 155), sprinkle with some mixed chia and sesame seeds, and serve with the quinoa and a few rye crackers on the side.

- FRIED EGG
- GINGER CARROT & PICKLED CUCUMBER
- WATERCRESS
- PUY LENTILS
- PRESERVED LEMON YOGURT
- FRESH MINT

FOR THE PICKLED CUCUMBER Thinly slice 1 cucumber and place in a heatproof bowl. Pour 235ml (8 fl. oz/1 cup) apple cider vinegar and 400ml (14 fl. oz./1¾ cups) water into a pan, then add 3 cracked cardamom pods and ½ tbsp sea salt. Add 1 tbsp coconut sugar for sweetness, if you like. Bring to the boil and simmer for 3–4 minutes before pouring over the cucumber. Cool to room temperature and refrigerate in an airtight jar (it keeps for up to 1 month).

FOR THE PUY LENTILS Heat a little olive oil in a pan and soften ½ small chopped onion, then add 55g (2 oz./¼ cup) Puy lentils, stirring for a minute before adding plenty of hot vegetable stock (to cover generously). Simmer for about 30 minutes until cooked but still with a little bite, then drain.

FOR THE GINGER CARROT Scrub 1 carrot, grate or julienne it and mix with ½ tsp grated fresh ginger and a squeeze of lemon juice.

FOR THE PRESERVED LEMON YOGURT Add ½ tsp finely chopped preserved lemon to 1 heaped tbsp natural (plain) yogurt and stir through.

FOR THE FRIED EGG Heat a little olive oil in a frying pan and fry 1 egg.

TO ASSEMBLE THE BOWL Add the lentils to the bowl, then a few slices of pickled cucumber, the ginger carrot and the fried egg. Add some watercress and chopped fresh mint and serve with the lemon yogurt.

SESAME TOFU
GREEN BEANS
MIXED CRESS
BUCKWHEAT NOODLES
TAHINI DRESSING

FOR THE TAHINI DRESSING Mix together the juice of 1 lime, 1 tsp coconut sugar, 1 finely chopped garlic clove, 1 tbsp fish sauce, 1 heaped tbsp tahini, 1 tsp almond butter, and 1 tsp chili oil, adding water as needed to give the desired consistency.

FOR THE SESAME TOFU Toss 120g (4 oz./1 cup) cubed firm tofu (beancurd) in 2 tbsp of sesame seeds.

FOR THE BUCKWHEAT NOODLES Cook 85g (3 oz.) buckwheat noodles for 5 minutes, or according to the instructions on the packet, then drain, and rinse in cold water.

FOR THE GREEN BEANS Steam 100g (3½ oz.) fresh green beans until cooked but still with a nice bite, drain, and refresh in cold water. Heat 1 tsp coconut oil in a wok or pan and add the beans to heat through.

TO ASSEMBLE YOUR BOWL Place the tofu, noodles, and beans in your bowl, and add some mixed cress. Serve with the tahini dressing, stirring everything together in the bowl.

MISO AUBERGINE
CRISPY SHALLOTS
PEA SHOOTS
BROWN RICE
TOFU ALMOND CREAM

FOR THE MISO AUBERGINE Mix 100g (3½ oz./6 tbsp) white miso soybean paste, 55g (2 oz./¼ cup) coconut sugar, 2 tbsp sake, and 2 tbsp mirin in a large pan and heat for a few minutes. Preheat the oven to 230°C/450°F/gas mark 8. Slice an aubergine (egg plant) into 3cm (1¼ in.) thick discs and toss in a bowl with a good glug of olive oil. Spread the slices out over a baking tray, brush generously with the miso mixture and roast in the oven for 15–20 minutes, turning the slices over halfway through and brushing the other side with the miso, until a rich golden colour and soft in the middle.

FOR THE CRISPY SHALLOTS Finely slice a couple of shallots and spread out over a baking tray. Drizzle with olive oil and roast in the hot oven alongside the aubergine for 20 minutes, until golden and crispy.

FOR THE BROWN RICE Cook 55g (2 oz./¼ cup) long-grain or brown rice according the instructions on the packet.

FOR THE TOFU ALMOND CREAM Blend 55g (2 oz./½ cup) smoked (or regular) soft tofu (beancurd) with some almond milk until creamy. Spoon into a small bowl.

TO ASSEMBLE YOUR BOWL Put the miso aubergine in the bowl and add the crispy shallots. Dollop over some tofu almond cream, top with pea shoots, and serve with the rice.

●● NORI FETA

● PICKLED SEAWEED

● CAVOLO NERO

● SPIRULINA RICE

● MICRO LEAVES

FOR THE PICKLED SEAWEED Put a few sheets of dried kelp or seaweed spaghetti into a pickling jar. Put 200ml (6¼ fl. oz./¾ cup) apple cider vinegar, 415ml (14 fl. oz/1¾ cups) water, and 55g (2 oz./¼ cup) coconut sugar into a pan, bring to the boil then pour over the seaweed in the jar. Leave to cool to room temperature, then close the jar. The pickled seaweed is ready to use once cool but will also keep in the refrigerator for up to 6 weeks.

FOR THE SPIRULINA RICE Cook 55g (2 oz./¼ cup) long-grain or brown rice according the instructions on the packet, then stir through 1 tsp spirulina powder.

FOR THE NORI FETA Cut 55g (2 oz./½ cup) feta into cubes and sprinkle with nori flakes.

FOR THE CAVOLO NERO Remove the woody stems from a few large leaves, then shred, rinse, and stir-fry in a little sesame oil in a wok.

TO ASSEMBLE YOUR BOWL Spoon the rice, nori feta, pickled seaweed, and cavolo nero into the bowl and top with micro leaves.

● PERSIAN CHICKEN SKEWERS
●●● GYPSY SALAD
● RED RICE
● TAMARIND YOGURT

FOR THE PERSIAN CHICKEN SKEWERS Marinate 1 large or 2 small boneless, skinless chicken thighs per person in a mixture of ground ginger, allspice, turmeric and cumin, crushed garlic, a little olive oil and some lemon juice, ideally overnight in the refrigerator. Cut the marinated thighs into smaller pieces and thread onto skewers before grilling for a few minutes on each side until cooked through.

FOR THE RED RICE Cook 55g (2 oz./¼ cup) red rice per person, according to the instructions on the packet.

FOR THE GYPSY SALAD Mix together grated carrot and fennel, with some chopped fennel fronds, chopped dried apricots, and toasted flaked almonds. Add a little sea salt.

FOR THE TAMARIND YOGURT Mix 1 tsp tamarind paste (loosened in a little hot water if very thick) into some natural (plain) yogurt. Toss the salad in a little of the tamarind yogurt.

TO ASSEMBLE YOUR BOWL Add the rice and salad to the bowl, top with the chicken, and serve with the rest of the tamarind yogurt.

ZA'ATAR SOYBEANS
RAW TOMATO SAUCE
SPINACH & BASIL LEAVES
RICE & QUINOA SPAGHETTI
PRESERVED LEMON DRESSING

FOR THE ZA'ATAR SOYBEANS Soak 55g (2 oz./⅓ cup) dried soybeans overnight, then drain, rinse, and pat dry. Mix with a little olive oil and 1 tsp za'atar. Sauté in a frying pan until golden. Add to a mixing bowl.

FOR THE RAW TOMATO SAUCE Roughly chop 8–10 heritage cherry tomatoes and add to the soybeans in the mixing bowl, along with a generous splash of tinned coconut milk.

FOR THE SPINACH & BASIL Roughly chop a large handful each of baby spinach and basil, and add to the mixing bowl.

FOR THE RICE & QUINOA SPAGHETTI Cook 85g (3 oz.) rice and quinoa spaghetti according to the instructions on the packet, then add to the mixing bowl and gently mix everything together.

FOR THE PRESERVED LEMON DRESSING Mix together the finely chopped rind of 1 preserved lemon, 1 finely chopped shallot, ½ tsp coconut sugar, and a good pinch of sea salt. Add 1 part white wine vinegar to 3 parts extra virgin olive oil, to make a thick dressing.

TO ASSEMBLE YOUR BOWL Add the soybean, spaghetti, and salad mixture to the bowl and drizzle over some preserved lemon dressing.

- CHOPPED EGG
- ASPARAGUS & SAMPHIRE
- BABY SPINACH
- BLACK QUINOA
- MUSTARD OLIVE OIL DRESSING
- RADISHES

FOR THE BLACK QUINOA Cook 40g (1½ oz./¼ cup) black quinoa in plenty of water for 20 minutes, then drain and return to the pan. Cover with a dish towel and the lid and leave to sit for 10 minutes. Add to a mixing bowl.

FOR THE ASPARAGUS & SAMPHIRE Snap off the woody ends of a handful of asparagus spears (about 100g/3½ oz.), chop into 5cm (2 in.) lengths and cut any that are thick in half lengthways. Rinse a good handful of samphire. Blanch the asparagus for 30 seconds in a pan of boiling water, then drain. Heat a wok or pan and add a little butter. Once hot, add the drained asparagus and cook for a couple of minutes before adding the samphire. Cook for a couple of minutes more, then tip into the mixing bowl.

FOR THE CHOPPED EGG & SPINACH Add an egg in its shell to a pan of boiling water and simmer for 9 minutes. Cool under running water, then peel, chop, and add to the mixing bowl with a large handful of shredded baby spinach.

FOR THE RADISHES Finely slice a handful of mixed radishes and add to the mixing bowl.

FOR THE MUSTARD OLIVE OIL DRESSING Mix together 1 tsp Dijon mustard and 2 tbsp lime juice or balsamic vinegar, 6 tbsp extra virgin olive oil, and plenty of seasoning. Add 2 tbsp to the ingredients in the mixing bowl and mix through, adding more if needed.

TO ASSEMBLE YOUR BOWL Add the dressed salad to the bowl.

- SALT & PEPPER TOFU
- BRUSSELS SPROUTS & BROCCOLI
- SPROUT FLOWERS
- BULGUR WHEAT
- LIME & SESAME DRESSING

FOR THE BRUSSELS SPROUTS & BROCCOLI Finely slice a handful of raw Brussels sprouts, using a mandolin or very sharp knife. Cut a third of a broccoli head into small florets. (You can steam the veg for a few minutes then refresh in iced water if you struggle to eat raw green vegetables.)

FOR THE SPROUT FLOWERS (or use shredded kale) Rinse and sauté in a little coconut oil.

FOR THE SALT & PEPPER TOFU Slice 100g (3½ oz./¾ cup) firm tofu (beancurd) into rectangular slabs. Crush 1 tsp mixed peppercorns (black, pink, green, and Sichuan) in a pestle and mortar and mix with ½ tsp flaky sea salt and 3 tsp cornflour. Coat the tofu slices in the seasoned flour and shallow-fry in a pan with very hot groundnut oil.

FOR THE BULGUR WHEAT Simmer 55g (2 oz./¼ cup) bulgur wheat in water with 1 tsp vegetable bouillon until cooked. Drain.

FOR THE LIME & SESAME DRESSING Mix together 3 tbsp toasted sesame oil, 1 tsp sesame seeds, the juice of 1 lime, a splash of fish sauce, and 1 tsp coconut sugar.

TO ASSEMBLE YOUR BOWL Cover the base of the bowl with bulgar wheat, then add the sprout flowers or kale. Toss the vegetables in some of the dressing and add to the bowl, then top with the salt and pepper tofu, and serve with more dressing.

- RED LENTIL HUMMUS
- RED BELL & CHILI PEPPERS
- WATERCRESS
- CAMOMILE BAKED SWEET POTATO
- OLIVE OIL DRESSING
- YEAST FLAKES

FOR THE CAMOMILE BAKED SWEET POTATO Preheat the oven to 190°C/375°F/gas mark 5. Spread 1 tbsp camomile flowers (loose tea) over the base of a small roasting dish and place 1 scrubbed sweet potato in the dish. Add water to come a third of the way up the potato, cover with foil and bake for about 45 minutes or until you can pierce the potato easily with a sharp knife. Remove from the oven and turn the oven up to 230°C/450°CF/gas mark 8. Carefully halve the sweet potato lengthways and transfer to an ovenproof griddle pan or skillet. Dot a little butter on top, then drizzle over 1 tbsp runny honey. Roast in the hot oven for 10 minutes, basting halfway through. Allow the potato to cool a little before cutting into wedges.

FOR THE RED LENTIL HUMMUS Cook 100g (3½ oz./½ cups) dried red split lentils in water and drain. When cool, add to a food processor and pulse until quite smooth before adding 1 small crushed garlic clove, the juice of 1 small lemon, 1 tbsp tahini, and ¼ tsp sea salt. Blend to a soft hummus texture, adding water as needed. Taste for seasoning and to check if you have enough lemon juice.

FOR THE RED BELL PEPPER & CHILI PEPPER Deseed and thinly slice 1 red bell pepper and ½ red chili pepper.

TO ASSEMBLE YOUR BOWL Add a couple of heaped spoonfuls of the lentil hummus and arrange the sweet potato wedges on top. Scatter over the bell pepper and chili pepper, a good handful of watercress, and some yeast flakes. Drizzle over just a little extra virgin olive oil and a pinch of flaky sea salt to serve.

- SOFT GOAT CHEESE
- PEACH, ORANGE, & PINK GRAPEFRUIT
- MUSTARD LEAF & FENNEL FRONDS
- TOASTED QUINOA
- POMEGRANATE OLIVE OIL DRESSING
- POMEGRANATE SEEDS

FOR THE TOASTED QUINOA Soak 40g (1½ oz./¼ cup) quinoa for a few minutes then tip into a sieve and rinse through. Heat a dry saucepan and add the quinoa, toasting until the grains separate and become fragrant, then add water or stock to cover, bring to the boil, and then reduce to a low simmer. Cover and cook for 15–20 minutes, then drain and return the quinoa to the pan, cover with a dish towel and the lid, and leave to sit for 10 minutes before adding to a mixing bowl.

FOR THE PEACH, ORANGE, & PINK GRAPEFRUIT Halve and stone a peach, cut into slices, and add to the mixing bowl. Peel and segment an orange and ½ pink grapefruit and add to the mixing bowl.

FOR THE MUSTARD LEAF & FENNEL FRONDS Add a good handful of mustard (or other) leaves and fennel fronds to the mixing bowl.

FOR THE POMEGRANATE OLIVE OIL DRESSING Mix together some extra virgin olive oil, pomegranate molasses (or honey), and sherry vinegar, to taste. Drizzle a little over the salad in the bowl and gently mix together.

TO ASSEMBLE YOUR BOWL Place the dressed salad in the bowl. Top with some soft goat cheese and scatter over pomegranate seeds.

- ORANGE BLOSSOM YOGURT
- CAULIFLOWER & FENNEL CRUDITÉS
- CHICORY & RADICCHIO LEAVES
- POLENTA CHIPS
- BLACK SESAME SEEDS
- DUKKAH SPICE MIX

FOR THE POLENTA CHIPS Pour 120ml (4 fl. oz./8 tbsp) milk and 120ml (4 fl. oz./8 tbsp) water into a pan. Place over a high heat and pour in 55g (2 oz./⅓ cup) quick-cook polenta (cornmeal), whisking as you do so to separate the grains. Bring to the boil then reduce to a simmer, stirring until it reaches a creamy consistency. Remove from the heat and stir in 1 tbsp finely grated Parmesan. Line a rectangular or square plastic container with baking parchment rubbed with oil. Pour in the polenta, cover the surface of the polenta tightly with plastic wrap, prick with the tip of a sharp knife, and leave to set overnight. Tip out the set polenta and cut into thick chips. Mix together some dry polenta and crushed peppercorns, then roll the chips in the mixture to coat on all sides. Heat some olive oil in a frying pan and fry the polenta chips until golden on all sides.

FOR THE ORANGE BLOSSOM YOGURT Mix 3 tbsp natural (plain) yogurt with 1 tsp orange blossom water. Spoon into a small dish and sprinkle over some black sesame seeds to cover one half.

FOR THE CRUDITÉS Chop some cauliflower, thinly slice some fennel, separate out some chicory and radicchio leaves. Sprinkle over a pinch of dukkah spice mix.

TO ASSEMBLE YOUR BOWL Add some chicory and radicchio leaves to the bowl, with some polenta chips and crudités. Serve with the orange blossom yogurt and black sesame seeds.

- GOAT CURD
- BAKED BEETROOT
- MIXED SALAD LEAVES
- SPROUTED BUCKWHEAT
- DILL DRESSING
- SWEET POTATO CRISPS

FOR THE BAKED BEETROOT Preheat the oven to 200°C/400°F/gas mark 6. Wash a couple of medium beetroot (beets) in a mixture of colours, if you like, and trim off the stalks to about 2.5cm (1 in.). Place in a roasting tray and pour over a 2 tbsp apple cider vinegar. Pour about a 2.5cm (1 in.) depth of water around the bottom of the beetroot and cover with foil, then bake in the oven for about 45–60 minutes, until you can pierce one easily with a sharp knife. Allow to cool a little before rubbing off the outer skin and cutting them into quarters.

FOR THE SWEET POTATO CRISPS Thinly slice a sweet potato, ideally using a mandolin, spread out on a baking tray and bake in the oven at 180°C/350°F/gas mark 4 until crisp, about 10–15 minutes.

FOR THE BUCKWHEAT Either buy sprouted buckwheat that is ready to eat, or rinse 40g (1½ oz./¼ cup) roasted buckwheat and cook for 10–15 minutes in a pan of simmering water before draining.

FOR THE DILL DRESSING Mix together 2 tbsp raspberry or white balsamic vinegar and 6 tbsp extra virgin olive oil with plenty of finely chopped dill and a little sea salt. In a large mixing bowl, mix together some salad leaves, the baked beetroot, and a couple of tablespoons of the dressing.

TO ASSEMBLE YOUR BOWL Add the dressed beetroot and a generous handful of mixed salad leaves to the bowl, then top with some goat curd, the buckwheat, and scatter over the sweet potato crisps.

●● LIME RICOTTA
● BABY CARROTS & WATERMELON RADISH
● LAMB'S LETTUCE & FENNEL FRONDS
● PEARLED SPELT
● CARROT JUICE DRESSING

FOR THE ROASTED CARROTS Preheat the oven to 200°C/400°F/gas mark 6. Scrub 100g (3½ oz.) baby carrots and trim the greens. Toss half the carrots in a little olive oil, cumin seeds, and salt and roast in the oven for about 20 minutes, until beginning to caramelise. Sprinkle over a little white balsamic or sherry vinegar and allow to cool. Leave the other half raw.

FOR THE PEARLED SPELT Bring a pan of water to the boil, add 40g (1½ oz./¼ cup) pearled spelt and simmer for about 20 minutes until cooked, then drain.

FOR THE LIME RICOTTA Mix the finely grated zest of ½ lime with 40g (1½ oz./¼ cup) ricotta.

FOR THE LAMB'S LETTUCE & WATERMELON RADISH Rinse a big handful of lamb's lettuce and thinly slice a watermelon radish or a few breakfast radishes.

FOR THE CARROT JUICE DRESSING Either juice a carrot or use cold-pressed carrot juice. Add a little carrot juice to the roasted and raw carrots, lamb's lettuce, watermelon radish, and pearled spelt, and gently toss together.

TO ASSEMBLE YOUR BOWL Put the tossed ingredients into the bowl and add a couple of spoonfuls of the lime ricotta, a few fennel fronds, and sea salt to taste.

- LABNEH
- RAW & ROASTED BEETROOT
- BABY CHARD & BEETROOT LEAVES
- RED RICE
- CHIA SEEDS
- BEETROOT DRESSING

FOR THE LABNEH Strain some thick natural (plain) or Greek yogurt through a muslin cloth suspended over a bowl overnight in the refrigerator, to leave a thick yogurt (you can use the whey liquid left over for tenderising meat or adding to smoothies).

FOR THE BEETROOT Preheat the oven to 200°C/400°F/gas mark 6. Wash a couple of medium beetroot (beets) and trim off the stalks to about 2.5cm (1 in.). Place in a roasting tray and pour over 2 tbsp apple cider vinegar. Pour a 2cm (¾ in.) depth of water around the bottom of the beetroot and cover with foil, then bake in the oven for 45–60 minutes, until you can pierce one easily with a sharp knife. Allow to cool a little before rubbing off the outer skin. Chop one into quarters and mash or process the other to a textured dip consistency. Hang the chopped beetroot in a muslin cloth over a bowl to collect the juice. Prepare a handful of raw baby beetroot by washing thoroughly and slicing in half lengthways, leaving the leaves intact if they are still bright-looking.

FOR THE RED RICE Bring a pan of water to the boil, add 40g (1½ oz./¼ cup) red rice and simmer, uncovered, for 30–40 minutes until cooked. Drain, return to the pan, cover with a dish towel and lid for a few minutes.

FOR THE BABY CHARD & BEETROOT LEAVES Simply rinse a good handful of baby chard and beetroot leaves (beet greens) or mixed leaf salad.

FOR THE BEETROOT DRESSING Mix the beetroot juice collected with 1 tbsp raspberry vinegar and 3 tbsp extra virgin olive oil.

TO ASSEMBLE YOUR BOWL Add the rice, roasted beetroot pieces, mashed beetroot, and the raw baby beetroot to the bowl and serve with the labneh and beetroot dressing. For extra crunch, scatter over chia seeds.

MACKEREL FILLET
CUCUMBER & MELON SALAD
LAMBS LETTUCE & MIXED HERBS
SUSHI RICE
OLIVE OIL DRESSING
SPELT FLATBREAD

FOR THE SUSHI RICE Cook 55g (2 oz./¼ cup) sushi or Thai sticky rice according to the instructions on the packet, leaving the lid on for 10 minutes after cooking to continue to steam. Stir through some chopped spring onion (scallion) and furikake (a Japanese seasoning of black and white sesame seeds and nori flakes) or sesame seeds.

FOR THE HERB CUCUMBER & MELON SALAD If you can find cucamelons, which have a flavour of melon and cucumber and look like tiny watermelons, slice a handful lengthways. (If you can't find cucamelons, use diced honeydew or galia melon.) Mix with ½ chopped cucumber, 1 finely chopped shallot, chopped fresh coriander, mint and parsley, and some toasted coriander seeds. Mix with a little hemp or extra virgin olive oil and season with sea salt and freshly ground black pepper.

FOR THE SPELT FLATBREAD To make 4 flatbreads, mix 125g (4½ oz./1 level cup) wholemeal spelt flour with a good pinch of sea salt. Add 120ml (4 fl. oz./½ cup) water a little at a time, kneading until it forms a soft dough. Sprinkle a little more flour over your work surface and divide the dough in four, rolling into balls. Squash a ball onto the floured surface and roll into a thin disc. Heat a large dry frying pan and, once hot, place a flatbread in the pan and cook for a minute or so until it begins to bubble, flip over and cook the other side until golden. Repeat with the remaining dough.

FOR THE MACKEREL Heat a little olive oil in a frying pan. Pat a mackerel fillet dry and season the flesh before placing in the hot pan, skin-side down. Cook for a couple of minutes before flipping over and taking off the heat, allowing the fillet to finish cooking in the residual heat.

TO ASSEMBLE YOUR BOWL Add a flatbread and top with the mackerel and rice. Add some cucumber salad to the side and top with sprigs of lambs lettuce.

- SALMON TARTARE
- CUCUMBER
- SPINACH
- FARRO
- WASABI MAYONNAISE
- FRESH HERBS

FOR THE SPINACH & FARRO Bring a pan of water to the boil, add ½ tsp sea salt and 55g (2 oz./¼ cup) farro, reduce the heat and simmer for 30 minutes or until cooked. Drain. Shred a handful of spinach and mix through the cooked farro.

FOR THE WASABI MAYONNAISE Whisk together 1 egg yolk, ¼ tsp wasabi, ½ tsp sea salt, and 1 tbsp brown rice vinegar or sushi-su, then add 150ml (5¼ fl. oz.) olive oil drop by drop as you whisk vigorously to emulsify. Alternatively, mix a little wasabi into Greek yogurt.

FOR THE SALMON TARTARE Cut a 100g (3½ oz.) sushi-grade salmon fillet, from a quality fishmonger, into small, neat cubes.

FOR THE CUCUMBER Peel about 5 long, thin ribbons of cucumber using a swivel vegetable peeler, then cut about a third of the remaining cucumber into small cubes. Mix the cubed cucumber and the cubed salmon into the farro and spinach. Squeeze over some lemon or lime juice and mix in some of the wasabi mayo.

TO ASSEMBLE YOUR BOWL Brush some more of the wasabi mayo around the rim of the bowl and stick the cucumber ribbons around the edge. Fill the bowl with the salmon tartare, cucumber, and spinach and farro mixture, then garnish with marigold leaves or any fresh herb.

- SALMON SASHIMI
- SEA VEGETABLE SALAD
- ASIAN GREENS
- STICKY RICE
- TAMARI DRESSING
- FURIKAKE

FOR THE STICKY RICE Cook 55g (2 oz./½ cup) Japanese or Thai sticky rice according to the instructions on the packet, keeping the lid on and, once cooked, leaving the lid on for 10 minutes to continue to steam before mixing with a rice paddle or spatula.

FOR THE SALMON SASHIMI Slice 100g (3½ oz.) raw sushi-grade salmon into 5mm (¼ in.) slices.

FOR THE SEA VEGETABLE SALAD Soak 5g (¼ oz.)dried sea vegetable salad in water for a few minutes.

FOR THE ASIAN GREENS If you can find tatsoi, these are good raw, or soften bok choy in a hot wok with a little sesame oil until just wilted.

FOR THE TAMARI DRESSING Mix together 2 tbsp tamari (wheat-free soy sauce), ½ tsp grated fresh ginger, 1 tbsp brown rice vinegar, and 1 tbsp lime juice.

TO ASSEMBLE YOUR BOWL Add the sticky rice, salmon sashimi, sea vegetable salad and tatsoi or bok choy to your bowl and top with a few beansprouts, thin slices of red onion, some pickled ginger and a pea-sized dab of wasabi. Scatter over furikake (a Japanese seasoning of black and white sesame seeds and nori flakes) or sesame seeds. Serve the tamari dressing as a dipping sauce.

CRAYFISH RICE VERMICELLI
GRAPEFRUIT & MINT SALSA
GINGER KALE & FENNEL FRONDS
AVOCADO

FOR THE GRAPEFRUIT & MINT SALSA Peel and segment a pink grapefruit. Mix with some sweet chili sauce or 1 tsp freshly chopped chili pepper and 2 tbsp honey, 2 tbsp red wine vinegar, and plenty of freshly chopped mint leaves.

FOR THE CRAYFISH RICE VERMICELLI Mix 80–100g (3½ oz./½ cup) cooked and cooled crayfish (large shrimp) with 55g (2 oz./¾ cup) cooked and cooled rice vermicelli.

FOR THE GINGER KALE & FENNEL Rinse a large handful of kale, remove the thick stalks, shred, and sauté in a little coconut oil and chopped ginger. Allow to cool then season with sea salt and toss gently with the crayfish and rice vermicelli. Add some thinly sliced raw fennel and ½ diced avocado and check again for seasoning.

TO ASSEMBLE YOUR BOWL Add the crayfish and rice vermicelli salad to the bowl and serve with a few spoonfuls of the grapefruit and mint salsa.

SPICED CALAMARI WITH CRAB & SPINACH FILLING
EDAMAME SALAD
THREE GRAIN QUINOA
LIME OLIVE OIL DRESSING

FOR THE EDAMAME SALAD Blanch 100g (3½ oz./1 scant cup) fresh or frozen shelled edamame beans until cooked but still with a nice bite. Drain and mix with some extra virgin olive oil and a little sea salt.

FOR THE CRAB & SPINACH FILLING Mix some white crab meat with some shredded spinach and lime juice.

FOR THE SPICED CALAMARI Ask your fishmonger to clean a whole squid, or use squid rings (and serve the crab filling alongside). If using a whole squid, cut it in half lengthways and lay it out flat. Score diagonal lines across the surface and cut in half. Fill one half with the crab and spinach filling and roll it up into a cylinder. Slice the other half into strips and marinate in a rub of crushed pink peppercorns, sea salt, grated lime zest, and a little ground ginger all mixed together. Heat a griddle pan and add a little olive oil. When very hot, add the calamari strips and cook briefly until no longer translucent but still tender. Remove from the pan and gently place the filled squid in the pan. Cook, turning every 30 seconds, until no longer translucent.

FOR THE THREE GRAIN QUINOA Cook a mixture of white, red, and black quinoa according to the instructions on the packet. Drain, return to the pan, cover with a dish towel and the lid, and leave to stand for a few minutes to absorb any excess moisture. Fluff with a fork.

FOR THE LIME OLIVE OIL DRESSING Mix together some extra virgin olive oil and lime juice, to taste.

TO ASSEMBLE YOUR BOWL Cover the base of the bowl with the quinoa. Add the edamame salad to the bowl with a good handful of mixed leaves. Top with the filled calamari and seared calamari strips. Drizzle over a little lime olive oil dressing.

● GARLIC MUSSELS
●● SEA SPAGHETTI
● SALTY FINGERS
● RED RICE

FOR THE SEA SPAGHETTI Soak 15g (½ oz.) sea spaghetti in cold water for 30 minutes. Bring a pan of water to the boil, add the drained sea spaghetti and boil until tender. Drain and toss in a little melted coconut oil.

FOR THE RED RICE Rinse 55g (2 oz./¼ cup) red rice and add to pan of boiling water. Reduce to a simmer and cook for 30–40 minutes, or until tender. Drain.

FOR THE GARLIC MUSSELS Check through 500g (18 oz./about 15–20) mussels, discarding any open ones that don't close when tapped firmly. Scrub off any barnacles. Heat 1 tbsp olive oil in a heavy-based saucepan, add ¼ finely chopped onion and 1 finely chopped garlic clove and cook gently until soft. Pour in 50ml (1⅔ fl. oz./3½ tbsp) white wine, then tip in the mussels. Give them a good stir, cover, then remove from the heat. They will continue to cook and open in the residual heat.

TO ASSEMBLE YOUR BOWL Pick the freshly cooked mussels from their shells and put in the bowl, pouring over the broth from the pan. Add the red rice, sea spaghetti, and some salty fingers (a type of coastal plant vegetable) or watercress.

HEARTY BOWLS

When you need a bowl to keep you going on a workout day or to impress friends and family at the weekend, try our hearty bowl ideas. From seared duck with babaganoush to laksa lamb with coconut polenta, see what takes your fancy.

HOMEMADE PANEER
TANDOORI SALSIFY
BABY SPINACH
COCONUT DAL
BEANSPROUTS

FOR THE **HOMEMADE PANEER** (Or use feta) Bring 950ml (32 fl. oz/1 quart) whole milk almost to the boil (so that it begins to foam at the edges of the pan). Reduce the heat and add 3 tbsp lemon juice, stirring a couple of times. Remove from the heat and leave to stand for the curds to form. After about 10 minutes, strain the curds through a muslin-lined sieve. Bring the edges of the cloth together and squeeze the curds to remove any excess whey. Place a weight over the bundle, still in the sieve, for about 15 minutes, then transfer to the refrigerator. Once chilled, it is ready and will keep in the refrigerator for 2–3 days.

FOR THE **COCONUT DAL** Rinse 85g (3 oz./½ cup) dried yellow split peas and add to a pan with 235ml (8 fl. oz./1 cup) vegetable stock or water and ½ tsp ground turmeric. Bring to the boil then reduce to a simmer for 20 minutes. Heat a little coconut oil in a frying pan and add 1 tsp mustard seeds and a few curry leaves. After 30 seconds, when the aromas are being released, add ½ sliced onion and sauté for a few minutes until soft. Stir the onion mixture through the split peas along with 150ml (5 fl. oz./⅔ cup) reduced-fat coconut milk, continue to simmer until the split peas are soft.

FOR THE **TANDOORI SALSIFY** Cut off the root from 1 salsify and peel it, then cut into large batons. Boil for 5 minutes, then drain (you can also use cauliflower in the same way). Mix together equal parts of ground cumin, coriander, ginger, paprika, turmeric, sweet chilli, and sea salt, then add enough groundnut oil to make a brushable paste. Brush the paste over the salsify batons (keep the remaining paste in an airtight jar in the refrigerator). Heat a frying pan and sauté the salsify until golden.

FOR THE **SPINACH** Rinse 2 large handfuls of baby spinach and wilt in a pan with a small amount of coconut oil (or leave it raw).

TO **ASSEMBLE YOUR BOWL** Spoon in some coconut dal and add salsify batons and spinach to the bowl. Crumble over some paneer or feta and top with a few beansprouts.

● ● ● MARINATED FETA
   ● ROAST TOMATOES
   ● CAVOLO NERO
   ● SPICED BEANS
   ● LAND CRESS

FOR THE MARINATED FETA Gently fry ¼ tsp each of black onion and coriander seeds in 1½ tbsp olive oil to release the aromas. Add these to 55g (2 oz./½ cup) cubed feta, along with the frying oil, and stir well. Marinate in the refrigerator, overnight if possible.

FOR THE ROAST TOMATOES Preheat the oven to 200°C/400°F/gas mark 6. Put a string of cherry tomatoes on the vine onto a roasting tray and roast in the oven until just bursting, about 15 minutes.

FOR THE SPICED BEANS Heat 1 tbsp olive oil in a pan with ½ tsp finely grated lemon zest, add 1 chopped spring onion (scallion) and cook until softened. Add 55g (2 oz./½ cup) canned, rinsed chickpeas (garbanzo beans) and 40g (1½ oz./¼ cup) canned, rinsed borlotti beans along with ¼ tsp ground cumin and a pinch of chilli flakes. Warm through and taste for seasoning.

FOR THE CAVOLO NERO Remove the woody stalks from a handful of cavolo nero leaves, shred the leaves, and massage in some apple cider vinegar to soften.

TO ASSEMBLE YOUR BOWL Add the spiced beans, cavolo nero, and roast tomatoes to your bowl, crumble in the feta, scatter over some cress and finish with a squeeze of lemon juice.

GRIDDLED HALLOUMI
ROAST JERUSALEM ARTICHOKES,
BURST TOMATOES & ASPARAGUS
JASMINE RICE
HONEY LEMON DRESSING
PICKLED RED ONION

FOR THE ROAST JERUSALEM ARTICHOKES & BURST TOMATOES Preheat the oven to 220°C/425°F/gas mark 7. Wash 3 or 4 Jerusalem artichokes, sprinkle with a little sea salt, and roast whole for about 20 minutes, or until they can be easily pierced with a sharp knife. Turn off the oven. Mix a handful of datterini or cherry tomatoes in a little olive oil and place on a roasting tray in the oven after you have removed the artichokes. These will warm and slightly burst in the residual heat.

FOR THE JASMINE RICE Measure 40g (1½ oz./¼ cup) jasmine rice, rinse well, and add to a pan with 1.5 times its volume of water. Bring to the boil then reduce the heat and simmer for 15–20 minutes, uncovered, until cooked. Drain then return to the pan, cover with a dish towel and the lid, and leave to sit for a few minutes.

FOR THE ASPARAGUS Griddle 4–6 asparagus spears, with the woody ends snapped off, in a hot pan, until coloured and cooked, but still with a nice bite.

FOR THE HALLOUMI Griddle 3 slices of halloumi in a hot pan, for about 4 minutes on each side, turning every now and then, until golden on the outside and soft in the middle.

FOR THE HONEY LEMON DRESSING Mix together some lemon juice, a little honey, and some extra virgin olive oil.

TO ASSEMBLE YOUR BOWL Arrange the jasmine rice, Jerusalem artichokes, tomatoes, asparagus, and halloumi in your bowl, adding some pickled red onion (see page 155). Drizzle over the dressing.

- POMEGRANATE LABNEH
- BABY LEEKS
- BABY SPINACH
- MUJUDARA LENTILS & RICE
- PISTACHIOS
- POMEGRANATE SEEDS

FOR THE POMEGRANATE LABNEH Strain some natural (plain) yogurt through a muslin cloth into a bowl overnight in the refrigerator, to leave a thick yogurt (you can use the whey liquid left over for tenderising meat or adding to smoothies). Add a little pomegranate molasses to the strained yogurt, spoon into a small dish and sprinkle with some pomegranate seeds and chopped pistachios.

FOR THE MUJUDARA LENTILS & RICE Add 55g (2 oz./½ cup) Puy lentils, ½ peeled small onion and 1 tsp vegetable bouillon powder to a pan of water, bring to the boil then reduce to a simmer for about 25 minutes, or until the lentils are cooked and still have a little bite, then drain. In a separate pan, cook 55g (2 oz./½ cup) long-grain rice according to the instructions on the packet.

FOR THE BABY LEEKS & BABY SPINACH Heat a little butter or oil in a griddle pan and griddle 3 baby leeks until soft and lightly charred, about 7–10 minutes (or sauté 1 regular leek, sliced, in a frying pan). Mix the leeks with the lentils, a handful of shredded baby spinach, some pomegranate seeds, and chopped pistachios.

TO ASSEMBLE YOUR BOWL Add some rice first, then top with the lentil mixture. Enjoy with pomegranate labneh on the side.

- ROAST CHICKPEAS
- COURGETTE & SWEET POTATO
- SPINACH
- LONG-GRAIN RICE
- SOFT BOILED EGG
- CARROT PICKLE

FOR THE CARROT PICKLE Scrub 500g (18 oz.) small carrots and cut them into random batons. Mix together 1 tsp grated fresh turmeric, 1 tsp grated fresh ginger, 1 crushed garlic clove, 1 tsp chili paste, and the juice of 1 lime (first grate the zest and reserve) with a little olive oil. Heat a good glug of olive oil in a pan and add 1 tbsp cumin seeds, 1 tbsp black mustard seeds, the grated zest of 1 lime (from the one used for juice), and 12 curry leaves. As the aromas are released, after about 30 seconds, add the carrots and spice paste, stirring well. Meanwhile, heat 300ml (10 fl oz./1¼ cups) vinegar in a separate pan and add 1 heaped tbsp coconut sugar or light muscovado sugar. When the sugar has dissolved, add the vinegar to the carrots, stir, and bring to the boil before reducing to a simmer for 10–15 minutes until the carrots are cooked but still have a bite. Allow to cool then transfer to an airtight jar. The pickle will keep for up to 2 weeks in the refrigerator.

FOR THE SWEET POTATO Preheat the oven to 200°C/400°F/gas mark 6. Scrub 1 small sweet potato, rub with a little olive oil, and score with a sharp knife a couple of times. Roast on a tray in the oven for 40–50 minutes until cooked but not too soft. Allow to cool before chopping into bite-sized cubes, or simply cut in half.

continued…

FOR THE ROAST CHICKPEAS Rinse 100g (3½ oz./¾ cup) cooked or canned chickpeas (garbanzo beans) and pat dry, then toss in groundnut or olive oil, 1 tsp paprika, and some salt. Spread out in a roasting tray and roast for 20–30 minutes at 200°C/400°F/gas mark 6, until golden and turning dark in places.

FOR THE RICE Cook 40g (1½ oz./¾ cup) long-grain or brown rice according to the instructions on the packet, then drain.

FOR THE BOILED EGG Add an egg to a pan of boiling water and simmer for 6 minutes. Cool under running water, peel, and halve.

FOR THE COURGETTE & SPINACH Cut 1 courgette (zucchini) into batons and sauté in a little olive oil. Steam or sauté a handful of spinach just until wilted. Chop 1 spring onion (scallion).

TO ASSEMBLE YOUR BOWL Add the rice, sweet potato, roasted chickpeas, courgette, spinach, and spring onion to the bowl and top with a generous spoonful of pickled carrots and the egg.

MASSAMAN BEANS
CHERRY TOMATOES
CAVOLO NERO
PISTACHIO BROWN RICE
SAFFRON YOGURT

FOR THE PISTACHIO BROWN RICE Cook 40g (1½ oz./scant ¼ cup) brown rice according to the packet instructions, drain, and stir through 1 chopped spring onion (scallion) and ½ tbsp chopped pistachios.

FOR THE MASSAMAN BEANS Heat 200g (7 oz./1⅓ cups) canned borlotti beans, drained, in a non-stick pan, stirring through 1 tsp massaman curry paste.

FOR THE GREENS Steam a large handful of cavolo nero or any leafy greens, or massage them raw in apple cider vinegar, to soften.

FOR THE SAFFRON YOGURT Soak a pinch of saffron strands in a little just-boiled water. Stir the saffron water and softened strands into 2 tbsp natural (plain) yogurt.

FOR THE TOMATOES Slice a small handful of vine-ripened cherry tomatoes.

TO ASSEMBLE YOUR BOWL Add the massaman beans, pistachio brown rice, cavolo nero, sliced tomatoes, and saffron yogurt. Season to taste.

●● VEGETABLE TAGINE
● SWISS CHARD
● WHOLEWHEAT COUSCOUS
● YOGURT
● ROSEWATER

FOR THE VEGETABLE TAGINE (Enough for 4 servings) Preheat the oven to 175°C/350°F/gas mark 4. Scrub 1 carrot and cut into chunks. Peel ¼ butternut squash and ¼ medium celeriac and cut into roughly 2.5cm (1 in.) dice. Cut 1 small turnip, 1 parsnip, 1 aubergine (eggplant) and 1 medium courgette (zucchini) into roughly 2.5cm (1 in.) dice. Combine the following with 100ml (3⅓ fl oz./⅓ cup) olive oil: 1 tbsp sweet paprika, ½ tbsp ground ginger, ½ tbsp chilli flakes, ½ tbsp ground cumin, ½ tbsp ground coriander, the seeds of 4 cardamom pods, 1 crushed garlic clove, the juice of 1 lemon, ½ tsp flaky sea salt and some black pepper. Mix the spiced oil with all the vegetables except the courgette, making sure they are coated well. Heat a large flameproof casserole, add the spiced vegetables and sauté for a few minutes. Add a 425g (15 oz.) can of drained chickpeas (garbanzo beans), 250ml (8½ fl oz./1 cup) vegetable stock, and 1 tbsp tomato paste. Give a stir, cover, and put in the oven for about 10 minutes, then add the courgette and cook for another 20–30 minutes, until the vegetables are cooked and the flavours have all infused.

FOR THE COUSCOUS Put 55g (2 oz./⅓ cup) wholewheat couscous per serving into a heatproof bowl. Pour over just-boiled water so the grains are just covered and add a drizzle of extra virgin olive oil. Cover with a plate and, after 5 minutes, check the water has been absorbed. Fluff with a fork.

FOR THE SWISS CHARD Roughly shred a large handful of rinsed Swiss chard per serving, and massage in a little apple cider vinegar.

TO ASSEMBLE THE BOWL Spoon in some vegetable tagine, add the couscous and Swiss chard, sprinkle over a few drops of rosewater, and serve with natural (plain) yogurt.

GOAT MILK RICOTTA
ROAST SQUASH
MIXED LEAVES
GIANT COUSCOUS WITH
HEMP SEED PESTO
CITRUS-INFUSED OLIVE OIL

FOR THE GOAT MILK RICOTTA (or use regular ricotta) Place 1 litre (32 fl. oz./1 quart) goat milk and ½ tsp salt in a saucepan and heat until you start to see foam at the edges of the pan. Remove from the heat and add 3 tbsp vinegar or lemon juice. Stir just once or twice and leave to form curds. Let the milk stand for at least 5 minutes then strain through a muslin cloth. Depending on the consistency you desire, you can let the curds drain for between 5 and 20 minutes: 5 will result in a very soft ricotta and 20 will be drier. Transfer to an airtight container, allow to cool to room temperature, place the lid on to seal, and keep in the refrigerator for up to 5 days.

FOR THE ROAST SQUASH Preheat the oven to 200°C/400°F/gas mark 6. Place a small squash, acorn or harlequin variety, on a roasting tray and roast in the oven until charred on the outside and you can easily pierce it with a sharp knife, about 1 hour. When cool enough to handle, tear the squash in half, then scoop out the seeds.

FOR THE GIANT COUSCOUS WITH HEMP SEED PESTO While the squash is roasting, process a 55g (2 oz.) mixture of basil and baby spinach leaves, 1 garlic clove, 2 tbsp hemp seeds and 120ml (4 fl. oz./8 tbsp) extra virgin olive oil until you have the required consistency. Add lemon juice and sea salt to taste. Cook 55g (2 oz./¼ cup) giant couscous according to the packet instructions, allow to cool a little then mix with 2 tbsp hemp seed pesto. (Keep the remaining pesto in an airtight jar for 2–3 days in the refrigerator.)

TO ASSEMBLE YOUR BOWL Place the squash halves in your bowl and spoon 2 tbsp pesto mixture into the cavities. Top with some crumbled ricotta and drizzle over a little citrus-infused olive oil (see page 155). Add plenty of mixed leaves on the side.

MUSHROOM & TOFU BIBIMBAP
RAW VEGETABLES
BOK CHOY
BROWN RICE
FRIED EGG
GOCHUJANG SAUCE

FOR THE GOCHUJANG SAUCE Mix together 1 tbsp gochujang paste, 1 tbsp rice vinegar, 1 tbsp light soy sauce, ½ tsp coconut sugar, ½ tbsp sesame oil, ½ tbsp sesame seeds, and 1 finely chopped spring onion (scallion).

FOR THE BROWN RICE Cook 55g (2 oz./¼ cup) brown rice according to the instructions on the packet (about 30 minutes), then drain.

FOR THE TOFU Cut 85g (3 oz./¾ cup) firm tofu (beancurd) into cubes and sprinkle with black sesame seeds and flaky sea salt.

FOR THE MUSHROOMS, RAW VEGETABLES & BOK CHOY Sauté a handful of exotic mushrooms, such as enoki, in a little sesame oil. Shave 1 carrot into ribbons using a swivel peeler, or use a spiraliser. Finely slice 1 spring onion (scallion) and separate out the leaves of 1 baby bok choy.

FOR THE FRIED EGG Fry 1 egg in a little olive oil and place on top of the rice in the centre of the bowl.

TO ASSEMBLE YOUR BOWL Spoon the brown rice into the middle and top with the fried egg, in the very centre so that the yolk will stay exposed. Add the tofu, mushrooms, raw vegetables, and bok choy around the sides of the yolk, and serve with the gochujang sauce and kimchi (see page 155) on the side.

- CRUMBLED TOFU
- SRIRACHA TOMATO SAUCE
- SAUTÉED GREENS
- TOASTED MILLET
- HONEY CASHEWS

FOR THE HONEY CASHEWS Preheat the oven to 180°C/350°F/gas mark 4. Toss 100g (3½ oz./¾ cup) raw cashews in a little groundnut or olive oil and sea salt. Melt 3 tbsp coconut sugar with 2 tbsp honey and 1 tbsp water in a small pan over a low heat. Pour this over the nuts, mix well to coat, and spread them out on a roasting tray. Roast in the oven for about 20 minutes until golden, stirring halfway through. Allow to cool before roughly chopping a handful of nuts. Transfer the rest to an airtight jar.

FOR THE SRIRACHA TOMATO SAUCE Place a handful of tomatoes on the vine on a roasting tray, drizzle with olive oil, and sprinkle with sea salt. Roast in the oven at 190°C/375°F/gas mark 5 until just bursting, about 12 minutes. Leave until cool enough to take off the vine, then blitz in a food processor with 1 tbsp sriracha (hot chilli) sauce, or to taste.

FOR THE MILLET Heat a dry saucepan and add the millet to toast for a couple of minutes until the grains begin to brown. Add twice the volume of water as millet with ½ tsp vegetable bouillon powder and bring to the boil, then reduce to a simmer, cover, and cook for about 15 minutes until cooked and all the liquid has been absorbed. Remove from the heat and place a dish towel over the pan and then the lid, letting it sit for 10 minutes before fluffing with a fork.

FOR THE GREENS Heat ½ tsp coconut oil in a wok or pan and sauté a handful each of kale, spring greens, bok choy, and savoy cabbage. Stir through the millet.

FOR THE TOFU Crumble 85g (3 oz./¾ cup) firm tofu (beancurd) into the greens and millet, then mix through.

TO ASSEMBLE YOUR BOWL Add the cooked millet, sautéed greens, and crumbled tofu mixture to the bowl, then top with the chopped honey cashews. Serve with warm sriracha tomato sauce.

GIROLLE & SHIITAKE RYE RISOTTO
BABY CHARD
WET WALNUTS
PARMESAN SHAVINGS

FOR THE RYE RISOTTO Soak 55g (2 oz./¼ cup) dried rye or spelt grains in plenty of water overnight, then rinse and drain. Sauté ½ finely chopped onion in a little butter or olive oil, add the rye grains, and stir through for 1 minute. Meanwhile, heat 300ml (10 fl. oz./1¼ cups) chicken stock in a separate pan. Ladle half the stock into the rye grains and cook as you would a risotto, stirring often, and adding more stock as needed. Rye will have a nutty bite even when cooked, which will take about 1 hour.

FOR THE GIROLLE & SHIITAKE MUSHROOMS Clean 30g (1 oz.) fresh girolle mushrooms and 55g (2 oz.) fresh shiitake mushrooms, then sauté in 1 tbsp melted unsalted butter. Season with a little sea salt and, if you like, a pinch of yeast flakes.

FOR THE BABY CHARD Wilt a good handful of baby chard leaves in the same pan as the mushrooms were cooked in, or in a steamer.

TO ASSEMBLE YOUR BOWL Spoon the rye risotto into the bowl and place the wilted baby chard on top. Add the mushrooms, some wet walnuts (when in season), generous shavings of Parmesan, and a few sprigs of mustard leaves.

CHILLI CHICKEN
CORN & AVOCADO SALSA
DANDELION LEAVES
BLACK QUINOA
ZESTY SOUR CREAM

FOR THE CHILLI CHICKEN Preheat the oven to 180°C/350°F/gas mark 4. Marinate 1 boneless chicken breast (skin on) for 10 minutes in 2 tbsp natural (plain) yogurt mixed with the juice of 1 lime and a pinch of chilli flakes. Heat an ovenproof griddle pan until hot, add the chicken, and sear on both sides, then transfer to the oven for 8 minutes, until cooked through and tender.

FOR THE CORN & AVOCADO SALSA If using fresh corn, brush the kernels of a fresh cob with melted coconut oil and griddle until lightly charred all over. When cool enough to handle, stand the cob on its end and use a sharp knife to slice the kernels down off the cob. Alternatively, melt a little coconut oil in a frying pan and sauté 85g (3 oz./½ cup) frozen kernels (from frozen). In a large bowl, mix the sweetcorn with 1 small peeled and diced avocado, ½ deseeded and finely chopped green chilli, plenty of chopped coriander, a good pinch of sea salt, and some lime juice.

FOR THE QUINOA Cook 55g (2 oz./¼ cup) black quinoa (or any type of quinoa) according to the instructions on the packet and stir through 1 tbsp ponzu or light soy sauce.

TO ASSEMBLE YOUR BOWL Cut the chicken into slices and add to the bowl with the quinoa, corn and avocado salsa, and some dandelion leaves (or any salad leaves), then top with a dollop of sour cream or natural (plain) yogurt garnished with some grated lime zest.

- # LEMON ROAST CHICKEN
- # GRILLED ASPARAGUS
- # MIXED CRESS SALAD
- # BULGUR & QUINOA
- # CHICKEN CREAM

FOR THE LEMON ROAST CHICKEN Preheat the oven to 190°C/375°F/ gas mark 5. Rub the skin of a small chicken (1–1.25kg/35–44 oz.) with a halved lemon. Place the lemon halves in the cavity. Sprinkle sea salt over the skin and smear over some softened butter, then place the chicken on a wire rack in a roasting tin. Roast for 1 hour to 1 hour 10 minutes, until the juices run clear, then cover and rest for 5–10 minutes before carving three thick slices per bowl. (The remainder of the chicken can be wrapped and kept in the refrigerator for up to 3 days. Alternatively, remove the thighs before roasting and use them to make the Chicken Fattee on page 126).

FOR THE CHICKEN CREAM Take some trimmings from the roast chicken and blend in a food processor with equal quanitites of chicken stock and almond milk. You are looking for a thick, creamy consistency. Pass this through a sieve for a smoother texture and taste for seasoning, adding a little sea salt and white pepper.

FOR THE ASPARAGUS Snap off the woody ends of 6 asparagus spears, toss in a little olive oil and grill, turning as they cook.

FOR THE BULGUR & QUINOA Bring a pan of water to the boil, add a 55g (2 oz./¼ cup) mixture of bulgur and quinoa, then simmer for 12 minutes until cooked. Drain and return to the pan, cover with a dish towel and the lid, and rest for a few minutes before fluffing up with a fork.

TO ASSEMBLE YOUR BOWL Put some slices of chicken breast in the bowl, with the bulgur and quinoa alongside. Add the asparagus, top with a handful of mixed cress, and serve with the chicken cream on the side.

SPICE RUB CHICKEN
ZESTY BUTTERNUT SQUASH
ROASTED CABBAGE
SPELT COUSCOUS
MICRO LEAVES

FOR THE SPICE RUB CHICKEN Mix together 1 tbsp groundnut oil and ¼ tsp each of sumac, grated lime zest, thyme, and crushed peppercorns (pink or black). Rub this paste over 1 boneless chicken breast (skin on) and leave to marinate for a couple of hours. When the squash and cabbage are cooked (see below) heat an ovenproof frying pan (skillet) and place the chicken skin-side down in the pan to sear for a couple of minutes. Turn over and sear the other side, then flip it over to skin-side down again and place in the oven at 180°C/350°F/gas mark 4 (reducing the temperature after the squash) for 6–8 minutes, until cooked through and tender. Cover and rest for 5–10 minutes.

FOR THE ROASTED CABBAGE Preheat the oven to 200°C/400°F/gas mark 6. Cut a pointed cabbage in half lengthways and brush all over with olive oil. Put into a roasting tin, season with sea salt, and sprinkle over ½ tsp fennel seeds. Roast in the oven for 35–40 minutes, until the edges are beginning to char and the cabbage is tender.

FOR THE ZESTY BUTTERNUT SQUASH Cut ¼ butternut squash into cubes, removing the skin at the same time (you can cook the whole squash this way and enjoy the leftover in salads or blitzed to make a soup). Toss the cubes in 1 tbsp olive oil and 1 tsp finely grated lemon zest, plus a little sea salt. Transfer to a roasting tin and bake alongside the cabbage for 20 minutes, until golden and beginning to caramelise, turning the cubes halfway through.

FOR THE SPELT COUSCOUS Add 55g (2 oz./⅓ cup) spelt (or wheat) couscous to a bowl, pour over just-boiled water to cover the grains, add 1 tsp extra virgin olive oil, and cover with a plate. After 5 minutes, fluff with a fork and stir through a little seasoning.

TO ASSEMBLE YOUR BOWL Place the chicken, couscous, cabbage, and squash in the bowl, then add some salad and micro leaves.

- CHICKEN FATTEE
- SPICED AUBERGINE
- COLESLAW
- LITTLE GEM LETTUCE
- SOFT SEEDED TORTILLA
- LIME YOGURT

FOR THE CHICKEN FATTEE Rub 2 chicken thighs all over with a mixture of 1 tbsp sea salt, 1 tbsp brown sugar, and 1 tsp of creole spice mix (see page 155), then leave to dry-brine in the refrigerator for 1 hour or preferably overnight. Wash off the brine mixture and pat dry. Preheat the oven to 175°C/350°F/gas mark 4. Heat a little groundnut oil in an ovenproof frying pan and add the thighs, skin side down, to seal. Add 1 tsp butter to the pan and roast in the oven for 25 minutes, until cooked through. Allow to cool a little before pulling off the meat from the bone.

FOR THE SPICED AUBERGINE Chop an aubergine (eggplant) into small cubes and toss in olive oil and ¼ tsp each of fennel seeds, mustard seeds, cumin seeds, and sea salt. Spread out on a roasting tray and roast in the oven at 220°C/425°F/gas mark 7 for about 10 minutes.

FOR THE COLESLAW Finely grate 1 carrot, 1 small courgette (zucchini), and ¼ green cabbage. Squeeze the grated courgette to remove any excess liquid. Toss the grated vegetables in a little apple cider vinegar and extra virgin olive oil.

FOR THE LIME YOGURT Mix a little grated lime zest into thick natural (plain) yogurt.

TO ASSEMBLE YOUR BOWL Line the bowl with a soft seeded tortilla and add the chicken, aubergine, coleslaw, little gem or round lettuce leaves, and a spoonful of lime yogurt. Serve with a lime wedge to squeeze over.

● LIME ROAST POUSSIN
● LIME CARROTS
●●● GREEN TABBOULEH

FOR THE LIME ROAST POUSSIN Preheat the oven to 190°C/375°F/gas mark 5. Rub the skin of a poussin with a halved lime. Place the lime halves in the cavity. Sprinkle sea salt over the skin and smear over some softened butter. Transfer to a shallow roasting tin and roast for 40 minutes, until cooked through and tender. Cover and rest for 5–10 minutes.

FOR THE GREEN TABBOULEH Finely chop a handful each of mint and flat-leaf parsley, ½ cucumber and 1–2 spring onions (scallions). Mix with 1 tbsp extra virgin olive oil, sea salt, and freshly ground black pepper. Bring a pan of water to the boil, add 30g (1 oz./⅛ cup) bulgur wheat, reduce to a simmer and cook for 12–15 minutes, until just tender. Drain.

FOR THE LIME CARROTS Clean a good handful of baby carrots, still with stems attached if possible, cutting any thicker ones in half lengthways. Boil for a few minutes then drain. Mix ½ tbsp butter with ½ tsp finely grated lime zest, and melt in a frying pan. Add the carrots and sauté, continually basting them with the butter, until softened.

TO ASSEMBLE YOUR BOWL Put the herbs and bulgur into the bowl, either keeping them separate or mixing some or all of them together, with the poussin. Add the lime carrots.

- SEARED DUCK BREAST
- BABA GANOUSH
- HONEY ROASTED GRAPES
- SCARLET KALE
- BROWN RICE

FOR THE BABA GANOUSH Cook an aubergine (egg plant) directly over the gas flame, holding it carefully with long-handled tongs and turning as the skin chars on each side until the flesh is soft within. (You can place it under a hot grill if you don't have a gas flame, turning it as it chars.) When completely charred and softened, place the aubergine in a bowl and cover until cool – this makes them very easy to peel. Peel, remove the seeds and discard them. Crush 1 garlic clove to a paste with some sea salt. Mash the aubergine flesh with the garlic paste, adding lemon juice and extra virgin olive oil to taste.

FOR THE SEARED DUCK BREAST Score the skin diagonally, almost – but not quite – through, the skin. Rub a mixture of 1 part sugar to 1 part salt over the breast and dry-cure for 1 hour. Wash thoroughly and pat dry. Preheat the oven to 160°C/325°F/gas mark 3. Place the duck skin-side down in an ovenproof frying pan (skillet), place the pan on the hob and turn on the heat to fairly high. When the skin is seared and beginning to colour, turn the duck over and sear the other side. Turn it back over to skin-side down again and place in the oven for about 5–8 minutes, depending on the size. It is done when it just has a firm feel when pressed. Take out of the oven and rest for a few minutes before slicing.

continued...

FOR THE HONEY ROASTED GRAPES In an ovenproof frying pan (skillet), mix a small handful of black grapes with a little olive oil, a splash of sherry vinegar or white balsamic vinegar, and a spoonful of honey. Roast in a hot oven at 200°C/400°F/gas mark 6 for 10 minutes and then transfer to the hob and sauté until the grapes are bursting and you have a sticky sauce.

FOR THE BROWN RICE Cook 55g (2 oz./¼ cup) brown rice according to the instructions on the packet.

FOR THE KALE Steam 85g (3 oz./2 cups) kale, tough stalks removed and leaves roughly chopped, for a few minutes and season.

TO ASSEMBLE YOUR BOWL Add the rice to the bowl with the duck slices on top. Spoon the baba ganoush on the side and top with the kale and roasted grapes. Drizzle over any remaining sauce from the grapes.

- PAN-ROASTED GAME
- SOFT-BOILED EGG
- ● ● CAESAR SALAD
- SPELT CROUTONS
- ANCHOVY FILLETS

FOR THE PAN-ROASTED GAME Preheat the oven to 180°C/350°F/gas mark 4. Spatchcock a pheasant (serves 2) or a quail (serves 1) by cutting along either side of the backbone to remove it so the game bird lays flat. Rub a little lemon, olive oil, and sea salt into the skin. Heat an ovenproof frying pan (skillet) and add the game bird to the pan skin-side down. Let the skin colour nicely before adding a few cubes of unsalted butter and transferring to the oven for 8–10 minutes (still skin-side down) until cooked. Allow to rest.

FOR THE SPELT CROUTONS Cut a thick slice of spelt or rye bread into squares. Toss in olive oil and a little sea salt, spread out on a roasting tray and bake in the oven 180°C/350°F/gas mark 4 for 10–12 minutes, until crisp, turning them halfway through.

FOR THE SOFT-BOILED EGG Add an egg to a pan of boiling water and simmer for 6 minutes. Cool under running water, peel, and halve.

FOR THE CAESAR SALAD To make the dressing, mix 1 finely chopped marinated anchovy fillet and a few finely chopped capers with a spoonful of natural (plain) yogurt, ½ tsp Dijon mustard, and a squeeze of lemon juice. Taste for seasoning and toss a couple of handfuls of baby gem and other salad leaves in the dressing. Add some shavings of Parmesan and the croutons.

TO ASSEMBLE YOUR BOWL Add the Caesar salad and egg to the bowl, with the pheasant or quail. Top with a marinated anchovy fillet.

SLOW-COOKED CHASHU PORK
SUGAR SNAP PEAS
BOK CHOY
SOBA NOODLES
BEANSPROUTS & PURSLANE

FOR THE SLOW-COOKED CHASHU PORK (Enough for 4 servings.) Preheat the oven to 150°C/300°F/gas mark 2. Put a piece of pork shoulder, about 800g (1¾ lb.), in a flameproof casserole with 120ml (4 fl. oz./ ½ cup) light soy sauce, 250ml (8½ fl. oz./1 cup) sake, 250ml (8½ fl. oz./ 1 cup) mirin, 250ml (8½ fl. oz./1 cup) rice wine, 40g (1½ oz./3½ tbsp) coconut sugar, 1 thumb-sized piece fresh ginger, sliced, and 6 or 7 peeled, whole shallots. Bring to the boil on the hob, cover, and transfer to the oven for 4–6 hours.

FOR THE SOBA NOODLES Cook 85g (3 oz.) soba noodles per serving according to the instructions on the packet, drain, and then refresh in cold water.

FOR THE SUGAR SNAP PEAS & BOK CHOY Blanch 55g (2 oz./½ cup) sugar snap peas and 55g (2 oz./1–1½ small bunches) baby bok choy per serving for 1 minute.

TO ASSEMBLE YOUR BOWL Pull the pork into shreds and add some to your bowl with the noodles, sugar snap peas, and baby bok choy. Add a handful of beansprouts and some purslane (or pea shoots), then ladle over some of the broth from the pork dish.

- MISO PORK
- LIME SPRING GREENS
- SALAD LEAVES
- TURMERIC SWEET POTATO
- TOMATO MUSTARD

FOR THE TOMATO MUSTARD Heat some olive oil in a pan and add 1 crushed garlic clove and a 285g (10 oz.) can of tomatoes, with a little water and some sea salt. Cook until very soft, then stir through 1 tbsp Dijon mustard. Allow to cool before transferring to an airtight jar and storing in the refrigerator.

FOR THE TURMERIC SWEET POTATO Preheat the oven to 190°C/375°F/ gas mark 5. Scrub a sweet potato, chop into cubes, and toss with a little groundnut oil, ½ tsp freshly grated or ground turmeric, and ½ tsp mustard seeds. Spread out in a roasting tin and roast for 20 minutes, until golden and cooked, turning halfway through.

FOR THE MISO PORK Season a pork chop with sea salt. Heat an ovenproof ridged griddle pan, add a little groundnut oil and, when hot, sear the pork chop on both sides, giving it a quarter turn to create criss-cross griddle marks. Spread ½ tsp miso mixed with ½ tsp butter on the top of the chop and place the pan in the oven (at 190°C/375°F /gas mark 5) to cook for 8 minutes, or until just cooked through, basting halfway through. Cover and rest for 5–10 minutes.

FOR THE LIME SPRING GREENS Sauté a large handful of shredded spring greens in a little melted coconut oil, then mix through 1 tsp shredded preserved kaffir lime leaves from a jar.

TO ASSEMBLE YOUR BOWL Place the pork in the bowl with the sweet potatoes and spring greens on the side. Add some extra green salad leaves and serve the tomato mustard separately on the side.

SEARED SIRLOIN
RAW KOHLRABI
TURNIP TOPS
JASMINE RICE
SUSHI GINGER

FOR THE JASMINE RICE Measure 55g (2 oz./⅓ cup) long-grain jasmine rice, rinse well, and add to a saucepan with 1.5 times its volume of water. Bring to the boil, then reduce the heat to a simmer, cover, and cook for 15 minutes, until the water is absorbed. Remove from the heat and place a dish towel over the pan, replacing the lid, and allow to sit for a few minutes before fluffing the rice.

FOR THE SIRLOIN Season a sirloin steak with sea salt and heat a ridged griddle pan. Once very hot, sear the steak for 4 minutes on each side (for medium-rare), giving it a quarter turn after 2 minutes to create criss-cross sear marks. Remove from the heat and allow to rest in the pan while you heat up the grill. Add a knob of butter to the top of the steak and flash under the hot grill for a couple of minutes before transferring to a board to slice. Rest for a few minutes before slicing.

FOR THE TURNIP TOPS (or any greens) Rinse, trim, and sauté a handful of turnip tops in 1 tbsp melted coconut oil, seasoning with a little sea salt.

FOR THE RAW KOHLRABI & SUSHI GINGER Peel a young, fresh kohlrabi, cut into small cubes and put into a small bowl. Put a little sushi ginger in a second small bowl.

TO ASSEMBLE YOUR BOWL Spoon the rice into the bowl, place the turnip tops or greens on the rice, then the sliced steak on top. Serve with the kohlrabi and sushi ginger.

LAKSA LAMB
SPRING ONION & GREEN CHILLI
PURPLE SPROUTING BROCCOLI
COCONUT POLENTA
TOASTED PINE NUTS

FOR THE LAKSA LAMB Mix 85g (3 oz./scant ½ cup) minced (ground) lamb with 1 tsp laksa paste (see page 155) and leave to marinate for 30 minutes. Heat a little groundnut oil in a frying pan and fry 3 curry leaves for a couple of minutes before adding the minced lamb. Fry until the minced lamb is browned and cooked through, then add a little stock for it to continue simmering and softening for another 10–15 minutes. Stir through some chopped coriander (cilantro).

FOR THE COCONUT POLENTA Bring 80ml (2½ fl. oz./5 tbsp) coconut milk (from a carton, not a can) to the boil in a saucepan and stir in 40g (1½ oz./scant ⅓ cup) quick-cook polenta (cornmeal), whisking as you do so. Lower to a simmer and keep stirring until it reaches a smooth, creamy texture. Season with a little sea salt and freshly ground black pepper.

FOR THE TOASTED PINE NUTS Toast 1 tbsp pine nuts in a dry frying pan (skillet) until golden, shaking the pan every now and then.

FOR THE PURPLE SPROUTING BROCCOLI Steam until cooked but still with a little bite.

TO ASSEMBLE YOUR BOWL Spoon the coconut polenta into the base of the bowl, then add the laska lamb and purple sprouting broccoli. Sprinkle over the toasted pine nuts and top with some very finely sliced spring onion (scallion) and green chilli.

TEA-SMOKED TROUT
SOFT-BOILED EGG
MIXED KALE
BELUGA LENTILS

FOR THE BELUGA LENTILS Rinse 55g (2 oz./⅓ cup) black beluga lentils. Sauté 1 finely chopped shallot in a little olive or groundnut oil. Add 1 tsp mixed crushed cumin, coriander, and fennel seeds, and continue to sauté for 1 minute until the aromas are released. Add the rinsed lentils and stir for 1 minute before adding 200ml (6¾ fl. oz./¾ cup) hot vegetable stock. Bring to the boil, then reduce the heat and simmer for 30–40 minutes, until the lentils are tender. Drain, then stir through a little extra virgin olive oil, sherry vinegar, and sea salt.

FOR THE TEA-SMOKED TROUT Rub a mixture of 1 part brown sugar and 1 part salt over a raw trout fillet and dry-brine overnight in the refrigerator. Line the base of a stove-top smoker with equal amounts of uncooked rice and loose-leaf tea (Earl grey or green are excellent) and place the grill rack over the tea and rice. Place, uncovered, on the hob over a medium heat until it starts to smoke. Rinse the brine off the trout and place the fillet on the grill rack. Close the smoker with the cover, remove from the heat, and set aside for 20 minutes. Check to make sure the fillet is cooked and easily flaked.

FOR THE MIXED KALE Rinse a large handful of green and purple kale leaves, remove the tough stalks, and steam until wilted. Season with a little sea salt.

FOR THE SOFT-BOILED EGG Add an egg to a pan of boiling water and simmer for 6 minutes. Cool under running water, peel, and halve.

TO ASSEMBLE YOUR BOWL Spoon the lentils into the bowl with the flaked smoked trout. Add the wilted kale and some baby salad leaves, and top with the soft-boiled egg.

LIME & FENNEL SALMON
UMEBOSHI PLUMS
ASIAN GREENS
PLUM & BUCKWHEAT NOODLES

FOR THE PLUM AND BUCKWHEAT NOODLES Cook 85g (3 oz.) plum and buckwheat (or any favourite variety) noodles according to the instructions on the packet, drain and rinse in cold water, then toss in a little sesame oil, 1 tbsp ume plum vinegar, and ½ tbsp mirin.

FOR THE LIME AND FENNEL SALMON Mix 1 tsp fennel seeds with 1 tsp finely grated lime zest, spread out on a roasting tray, and gently dry in a low oven at 120°C/250°F/gas mark ½ for about 10 minutes. Remove from the oven and increase the temperature to 190°C/375°F/gas mark 5. Pan-fry a salmon fillet skin-side down in an ovenproof non-stick pan, for about 5 minutes, until the skin is crisp. Mix a little wasabi with 1 tsp grain mustard or white miso paste. Take the salmon off the heat, spread the wasabi mixture over the top (the non-skin side) then scatter over the fennel seeds and lime zest. Finish off in the oven for about 6 minutes, depending on how you like your salmon cooked.

FOR THE ASIAN GREENS If you can find tatsoi, these are good raw, or soften bok choy in a hot wok with a little sesame oil until just wilted.

TO ASSEMBLE YOUR BOWL Add the noodles, salmon, greens, and one or two umeboshi plums.

● ● HOT-SMOKED SALMON
● CELERIAC REMOULADE
● CUCUMBER RIBBONS
● MIXED SALAD LEAVES
● ● FARRO
● NORI OLIVE OIL DRESSING

FOR THE CELERIAC REMOULADE Peel and finely slice about ¼ medium celeriac per serving, ideally with a mandolin. Slice again into thin strips and marinate in milk for a couple of hours. Drain and mix with some natural (plain) yogurt, 1 tsp horseradish mustard, a little sea salt, a squeeze of lime juice, and a couple of drops of Tabasco sauce.

FOR THE FARRO Bring a pan of water to the boil and add a good pinch of sea salt and 55g (2 oz./¼ cup) farro. Reduce the heat and simmer for about 30 minutes until cooked. Drain and mix with a little extra virgin olive oil.

FOR THE HOT-SMOKED SALMON To smoke your own, rub a mixture of 1 part brown sugar and 1 part salt over a raw salmon fillet and dry-brine overnight in the refrigerator. Line the base of a stove-top smoker with equal amounts of uncooked rice and loose-leaf tea (Earl grey or green are excellent) and place the grill rack over the tea and rice. Place, uncovered, on the hob over a medium heat until it starts to smoke. Rinse the brine off the salmon and place the fillet on the grill rack. Close the smoker with the cover, lower the heat, and smoke for 10–15 minutes, depending on how rare you prefer your salmon in the middle. Allow to cool a little (or you can serve cold) before flaking.

FOR THE CUCUMBER RIBBONS Pare strips of cucumber, lengthways, using a swivel vegetable peeler. Season with a little sea salt and freshly ground black pepper.

TO ASSEMBLE YOUR BOWL Spoon the farro into the bowl and add the celeriac remoulade and flaked salmon. Add the cucumber ribbons and a good handful of mixed salad leaves. Serve with a dressing of extra virgin olive oil infused with 1 tsp nori flakes.

●● COCONUT SHRIMP
● PEAS
● PEA SHOOTS
● CONGEE RICE
● SHREDDED HERBS

FOR THE CONGEE RICE Put 100g (3½ oz./½ cup) short-grain rice (or brown), 3½ cups water, a couple of thick slices of fresh ginger, and a bashed lemongrass stick into a saucepan. Bring to the boil, then reduce the heat to a low simmer for about an hour, or until the rice has completely broken down. Remove the ginger pieces and lemongrass.

FOR THE COCONUT SHRIMP Marinate 85g (3 oz./¾ cup) raw shelled shrimp in 1 tbsp green Thai paste (see page 155) for 1 hour while the rice cooks. Heat 1 tsp sesame or groundnut oil in a wok, add the shrimp and then, after a couple of shakes of the wok, add 50ml (12/3 fl. oz./3½ tbsp) reduced-fat coconut milk. Cook the shrimp until they turn pink.

FOR THE PEAS Bring a small pan of water to the boil and add 85g (3 oz./⅔ cup) peas (fresh or frozen). Cook for a minute or two, then drain.

TO ASSEMBLE YOUR BOWL Add the congee rice to the bowl and then the prawns, peas, and a large handful of pea shoots. Scatter a few torn Thai basil leaves, coriander (cilantro) leaves, and shredded kaffir lime leaves over the top (optional). Mix it all through.

●● CRAB BARLEY BROTH
●● CRAB GYOZAS
● SPRING ONION
● SHREDDED CABBAGE
● PRAWN TOAST

FOR THE CRAB BARLEY BROTH Pick and set aside the meat from a freshly cooked crab, discarding the top shell and feathery cones (the lungs, which are the only toxic part of the crab). Place the picked lower shell piece, legs, and claws in a large saucepan, add some onion, roughly chopped celery, a peeled garlic clove, a couple of bay leaves, some black peppercorns, a sprig of thyme, and some sea salt. Cover with cold water, bring to the boil then reduce to a simmer, uncovered, for an hour, skimming away any white foam that comes to the top. Taste, and if you prefer a stronger flavour, simmer for another 20 minutes. Cool a little then strain through a fine sieve. Meanwhile, bring a pan of water to the boil, add 40g (1½ oz./¼ cup) barley per serving and cook for about 45 minutes or until tender. Drain and add to the crab broth.

FOR THE PRAWN TOAST Finely chop 10 raw prawns (shrimp) and mix with 1 egg white, whisked to a foam, 1 tsp sesame oil, ½ tbsp cornflour, 1 tbsp light soy sauce, 1 tbsp chopped coriander (cilantro) leaves, 1cm (½ in.) piece of fresh ginger, grated, and 1 finely chopped garlic clove. Spread thickly over a slice of sourdough toast, sprinkle with sesame seeds, and grill for about 5 minutes, then cut into 4 triangles.

FOR THE CRAB GYOZAS Mix the picked crab meat with sea salt, black pepper, and lime juice, then spoon a little into the centre of a gyoza wrapper (available in Asian stores). Mix a little cornflour with water and use this to stick the edges of the gyoza together, folding in half and pleating the edges by pinching between your fingers. Heat some groundnut oil in a pan and fry the gyozas on both sides until golden (or you can steam them in a bamboo steamer for 12–15 minutes).

FOR THE GREENS Shred some green cabbage and spring onion (scallion).

TO ASSEMBLE YOUR BOWL Spoon in the crab barley broth and top with pieces of prawn toast, gyozas, some greens, and sprigs of coriander.

STORECUPBOARD RECIPES

BUTTERMILK DRESSING

Mix together 3 tbsp buttermilk, 1 tsp Dijon mustard, a splash of white balsamic vinegar, ½ finely chopped shallot, and 2 tbsp extra virgin olive oil. Season with sea salt to taste.

PRESERVED LEMON DRESSING

Mix together the finely chopped rind of 1 preserved lemon, 1 finely chopped shallot, ½ tsp coconut sugar, and a good pinch of sea salt. Add 1 part white wine vinegar to 3 parts extra virgin olive oil, to make a thick dressing.

TAHINI DRESSING

Mix together the juice of 1 lime, 1 tsp coconut sugar, 1 finely chopped garlic clove, 1 tbsp fish sauce, 1 heaped tbsp tahini, 1 tsp almond butter, and 1 tsp chilli oil, adding water as needed to give the desired consistency.

TURMERIC DRESSING

Mix together ½ tsp freshly grated or ground turmeric, 2 tsp pickled mustard seeds and the pickling liquid (see below), 1 tsp runny honey, and 3 tbsp extra virgin olive oil.

CITRUS-INFUSED OLIVE OIL

Place 500ml (17 fl. oz./2 cups) extra virgin olive oil in a pan with the pared zest of 1 lemon or orange. Gently warm for 5 minutes. Allow the oil to cool before transferring to an airtight jar with the zest.

CREOLE SPICE MIX

Mix together 1 tbsp crushed pink peppercorns, 6 crushed kaffir lime leaves or 1 tbsp grated lime zest, ¼ tsp garlic powder, ½ tsp ground ginger, and 1 tsp dried thyme leaves.

GREEN THAI PASTE

In a food processor combine 50ml (1⅔ fl. oz./3½ tbsp) coconut cream, 1 tbsp coconut sugar, 2 green chillies, 1 lemongrass stalk, ½ thumb-sized piece of ginger, peeled, zest and juice of 1 large or 2 small limes, 6 kaffir lime leaves (optional), ½ tsp grated fresh or ground turmeric, 1 tsp coriander (cilantro) seeds, and 1 tsp cumin seeds. Store in an airtight jar in the refrigerator for up to 2 weeks.

LASKA PASTE

Heat a dry frying pan (skillet) and add 1 tbsp coriander seeds, 1 tbsp cumin seeds, and 3 star anise. Toast for a minute or so until the aromas are released, then grind in a spice grinder or pestle and mortar. Add to a small food processor with 1 deseeded and chopped red chili pepper, 55g (2 oz./½ scant cup) fresh ginger, peeled and roughly chopped, 8 kaffir lime leaves or the grated zest of 1 lime, 3 lemongrass stalks, and enough of a 1 part sesame oil to 1 part groundnut oil mixture to form a smooth, quite thick paste when blitzed. Store in an airtight jar in the refrigerator for up to 1 month.

KIMCHI

Shred the leaves of a Chinese cabbage and separate out the shreds. Toss in 1 tbsp sea salt, making sure the shreds are evenly covered, then leave to sit for a couple of hours before rinsing and draining. Mix together 40g (1½ oz.) Korean red pepper powder (gochugaru), 55g (2 oz.) anchovy sauce, and enough water to make a runny paste. Mix this with 1 tbsp grated fresh ginger, 1 crushed garlic clove, and a couple of sliced spring onions (scallions). Mix this into the cabbage, massaging the paste in well. Transfer to a sterilised jar so that there is a little liquid over the top of the cabbage. Seal and leave at room temperature for 1 day to kickstart the fermentation process, before storing in the refrigerator for up to 1 month. Open the lid every few days to relieve any pressure building up inside the jar.

PICKLED MUSTARD SEEDS

Heat 1 part apple cider vinegar to 2 parts water until boiling, then pour over mustard seeds in a pickling jar. Store in an airtight jar in the refrigerator for up to 1 month.

PICKLED RED ONION

Slice 1 or 2 red onions and blanch in boiling water. Drain and add to a pickling jar. Bring 100ml (3⅓ fl. oz./⅓ cup) apple cider vinegar and 50ml (1⅔ fl. oz./3½ tbsp) lemon or lime juice to the boil, add 1 heaped tbsp coconut sugar and 1 tsp mustard seeds. Stir until the sugar has dissolved. Pour over the sliced onions. Allow to cool to room temperature, seal the lid. Store in an airtight jar in the refrigerator for up to 2 weeks.

INDEX

Publishing Director: Sarah Lavelle
Commissioning Editor: Lisa Pendreigh
Copy Editor: Sally Somers
Creative Director: Helen Lewis
Senior Designer: Nicola Ellis
Recipe Writing, Additional Text, and
Food Styling: Food for Happiness
Photographer: Issy Croker
Prop Stylist: Polly Webb Wilson
Production Director: Vincent Smith
Production Controller: Tom Moore

First published in 2016 by
Quadrille Publishing Limited
Pentagon House
52–54 Southwark Street
London SE1 1UN
www.quadrille.co.uk www.quadrille.com

Quadrille is an imprint of Hardie Grant
www.hardiegrant.com.au

Reprinted in 2016 (twice)
10 9 8 7 6 5 4 3

Cataloguing in Publication Data: a catalogue
record for this book is available from the
British Library.

ISBN: 978 184949 798 5

Printed in China

The publisher would like to thank the following for
the loan of bowls, spoons, and linens for photography:

Pip Hartle
piphartle.com

Daisy Cooper
daisycooperceramics.com

Tom Butcher
tombutcherceramics.co.uk

Kana London
kanalondon.com

Hope in the Woods
hopeinthewoods.com

Sue Pryke
suepryke.com

Nick Membry
kitchen-pottery.co.uk

Andrea Roman
arceramics.co.uk

Pottery West
potterywest.co.uk

Alex Devol
woodwoven.com

The Linen Works
thelinenworks.co.uk